LET'S TALK
PARENTING

ESTHER • MARTHA
THOMAS • PETER
PAUL • JOSHUA
NAOMI • NEHEMIAH
MARY • HANNAH

10

Bible Characters
Every Family
Should Meet

DIANE OVERGARD
JANICE RUBIN

FAMILY IMPACT

Cover and text design, typography: Ragont Design

ISBN: 0-9720589-0-7

10 Bible Characters Every Family Should Meet

This book is lovingly dedicated to
our husbands, Mark and Jeff,
and to our children,
Chris, Josh, Brooke, Jami, Jessica, and Courtney.

INTRODUCTION

*W*orking with families for over twenty years in both church settings and the public sector, we have compiled key skills and attitudes that parents have told us made the greatest impact on their understanding of their children, and themselves. This book contains *specific skills* parents can develop through active learning experiences. As educators, we believe much is gained through self-discovery.

Parental attitudes also are explored in this text. Taking the time to clarify attitudes about children, parental roles and relationships can help parents make purposeful decisions in their interactions with their children. Our writing and teaching encourage parents to explore their own attitudes, hear some additional information, and then make choices that will be most effective in their own families.

From the very beginning we knew that we did not, and never will, have all the answers. What we do have is a list of good resources: books, trusted professionals, and God. Healthy families seek help when challenges arise. God is the best resource of all. He is always "on-call" to provide us with wisdom and encouragement. As parents, we can look to God to be our partner in raising our children.

Let's Talk Parenting: Ten Bible Characters Every Family Should Meet is ten chapters: perhaps ten weekly classes at church, or ten coffee mornings at home with neighbors, or just ten times to sit down and read this book alone. Each chapter begins with time to pull out a Bible and understand a theme presented through the life of a Biblical character. The parenting skills and attitudes that follow are reinforced by that theme. Each chapter includes opportunities for practice and reflection. To enhance the experience of a small group order the separate Leader's Guide which includes scheduling help, additional interactions, and tips for facilitators.

We are excited for the opportunity to share our work with you! Whether you are in a group setting, enjoying the connections and support or other parents, or reading on your own, it is our sincere wish that some little part of this book will make a positive difference in your relationship with your children, and in your relationship with God.

Diane Overgard
Janice Rubin

CHAPTER 1

ESTHER

God Has a Plan for ME As a Parent

IN THIS SESSION

Childhood Memories

I can remember...

- Playing hide and go seek in the dark
- Penny candy from the Dime Store
- Old Maid, Crazy Eights, and Monopoly
- Lunch boxes with a Thermos
- Simon Says and Mother May I
- Toboggans
- Making forts
- Backyard shows for the neighborhood
- Just sitting on the curb
- Jumping on the bed
- Laughing so hard your stomach hurt
- Paper chains at Christmas

I think my child will remember...

ESTHER

Esther
Chapters 1–10

When you look in the
Bible, characters such as Esther come alive with the clarity that
God truly does have a plan for our lives!

Her story begins in the royal palace of King Xerxes and
Queen Vashti. One day, "when King Xerxes was in high spirits
from wine," (Esther 1:10) he commanded the Queen to come
before him to display her beauty to the people and the nobles.
But Queen Vashti had a mind of her own, and refused! What
was King Xerxes to do about this? No one, not even the Queen,
could be allowed to disobey the King! Under the advice of his
wise men, King Xerxes decreed that Vashti was never again to
enter his presence. Soon after, a search began for beautiful
young virgins who might be suitable candidates to become
King Xerxes' new queen.

Esther was a Jewish girl whose mother and father had died.
She was being raised by her cousin, Mordecai. During the
King's search for a new queen, beautiful Esther was taken to the
palace, but since Jews were being highly persecuted at that
time, Mordecai warned her to keep her nationality secret. Esther found favor with the King and was named Queen. Imagine
a Jewish girl living her life in a palace!

As time passed, Queen Esther learned of a plot to kill all
the Jews, her own family line. Esther had to make a choice, but
not without relying on God's help. Esther's story illustrates
God's amazing design for each of our lives. Not only did God
have a plan for Esther, but he allowed her the opportunity to
make an important choice.

God had a plan for Esther's life. Search these verses for evidence of God working behind the scenes of Esther's life.

Read Esther 1:10–12, 15, 19, and 2:2
How did Esther have the opportunity to become Queen?

Read Esther 2:7–10
What special circumstances occurred in Esther's life? Why was it especially unusual for Esther to be chosen Queen?

> **When things happen in our lives that we do not understand, remember that God has a plan.**

When Esther learned of the plot to destroy the Jewish people, she had to make a choice.

Read Esther 4:12–14

What did Esther see as her options?

"Who can say but that God has brought you into the palace for just such a time as this?"
ESTHER 4:14

> **God has a plan for our lives but gives us opportunities to make choices.**

Esther chose to confront the King to plead for the lives of the Jews. There was danger in this because, in those days, it was against the law to approach the King without being summoned, and anyone doing so would be killed! Furthermore, Esther was to identify herself as a Jew and petition for the King to save all Jewish people. Esther sought God's wisdom by asking Mordecai and the Jews to join her in fasting and praying before she approached the King. (Esther 4:15–16).

With God's help, Esther was successful.

Read Esther 8:11 and 8:17 to see the outcome.

God can have great impact on lives when people seek His wisdom

God had a plan for Esther's life.

God has a plan for each of our lives!

Have you ever considered that God must have planned for this child to be born for you, especially you?

▼ ▼

"For we are God's workmanship, created in Christ Jesus to do good works, which God prepared in advance for us to do."'
—Ephesians 2:10

First there were... My Parents

How in the world did I get to be THIS kind of parent?

Things I do the same as my parents:

1.

2.

Our own parents provided for us our first role models of "how to be a parent." In some instances we copy our parents, and in other ways we may try to be their opposite. In any case, we learn much of our parenting philosophy from our parents.

Things I do differently from my parents:

1.

2.

God was at work even when I was a child, giving me the experiences to create the person I am today.

Were these intentional choices? Why or why not?

And then I observed Other Parents

Did you see that mom in the supermarket? >

We learn about parenting by watching other parents.

"Cory! I'm warning you to quit whining or you will get a spanking!"

"Connor, can you find the cat food for Whiskers on that low shelf?"

"Don't put your fingers in the hamburger!"

"I hear that you really want to buy candy but it's lunch time right now."

"Emily! Get over here!"

"Which apples look the best to you, Alex?"

"Do you have to touch everything you see?"

"I need you to help me count out six oranges."

"Don't tip over the cart!"

"I know it's hard to see all this food and not be able to eat it right now."

How have outside influences positively impacted my parenting?

CHOICES

Queen Esther was faced with a choice: Should she risk her life and her position by approaching King Xerxes and asking him to save the Jewish people? Or, should she pretend she didn't know what was planned, enjoy her position of favor with the king, and assume she would be protected even if her people, the Jews, were destroyed?

Just as Esther had a choice to make, we as parents have choices, too. Nearly all of us have been raised with a variety of parenting techniques: Some we want to copy, and others we try to avoid. We have all observed parenting strategies we admire, as well as some that make our hair stand on end!

God fills our lives with influential people and experiences. Every experience impacts us in some way, helping to develop within us our values and individual characteristics. Ultimately, the choice is ours to decide what type of parent we will become for our children.

Just as Esther had a choice, I can choose to be the most effective parent I can be.

Parents Are People

Parents are people
Who were once children.
Children, who got a fair shake, or a bad break.
Children, whose memories were vivid and impressionable.
Children, who learned to adapt to situations beyond their control.
Children, who have been influenced by words of kindness or ridicule.
Children, who keenly observed models of compassion or indifference.
Children, who have grown to become parents.

"Every experience God
puts in our lives, **every person
whom we encounter,** is the perfect
preparation for the future which only
He can see."

—Corrie ten Boom

"Protect Me Daddy"

The Knight in Shining Armor galloped his white horse at full speed to the castle, where a Damsel in Distress cried from her window, "Help! Help! Save me!" Within moments a dragon was slain, an evil stepmother was quieted, and an iron barricade was flattened. The Knight and the Damsel, no longer in distress, rode happily off into the sunset.

Throughout history, men have filled the role of protector. Men, from the Knight in Shining Armor to Superman, have confidently risen to this challenge. However, when these men become fathers and consider the many needs of children—physical, emotional, spiritual, and financial—it's not uncommon to feel anxiety in this new role of Daddy. In the early years, dads may have been able to confidently respond to the unspoken expectation of **"Protect me Daddy."** Later, feelings of helplessness may creep in when problems seem bigger. Consider the father trying to comfort and emotionally protect his sullen son who was not chosen for the soccer team that all the other friends had made. What about the father who arrived home finding his distraught daughter crying because her boyfriend just broke up with her. What's a father to do?

The importance of being a father is seen in the influence they have with their children. Daddy is the man who wrestles, laughs, tickles, tackles, cries and loves even when he is too weary to do so. Trusting the Father of all fathers to work His perfect plan is the best way to handle these circumstances and live our lives within our family.

When considering these tough situations and overwhelming feelings, there is great peace in knowing that God never meant for dads to go it alone. Human effort is inadequate but God's power is invincible. He is the great protector and even gave the image and gift of **The Armor of God** found in Ephesians 6:10–18.

The example fathers live and the instruction they can pass on to a child is to put on the full armor of God to be able to stand their ground. What does that entail? Putting on the belt of *truth* gives clarity to the confusion often faced. God's truth is available to all believers. With truth and honesty in a relationship there is trust. The shield of *faith* protects against anxiety, fear and worry. Having faith in God allows fathers to trust that God is in control and that earthly fathers don't have to have all the answers. Where do the answers come from? The sword which is the **Word of God.** This weapon can be used for the many challenges that occur. When decisions are based on God's Word, He can provide guidance. Armored with *truth, faith* and *God's Word,* families are able to stand firm.

"*Protect me Daddy*" is a prayer that may soon roll off lips with the assurance that raising a modern day knight is a goal worth pursuing!

GOD HAS A PLAN FOR ME AS A PARENT

God has molded us with memorable experiences and significant people in our lives. When we take the time to recognize those influences, and learn the lessons available there, we can make wise choices to become the people God intended us to be, as well as the parents God intended us to be for our children.

REFLECTIONS

Experiences and people God placed in my life have led to MY STRENGTHS...

Some experiences I'm carrying around as old baggage are MY CHALLENGES...

God had a plan for Esther's life and gave her choices to make. God has a plan for my life and gives me choices to make. **As a parent, one choice I'd like to make today is:**

IMPACT MY FAMILY

Let's Talk

This section extends this curriculum to include additional family members.

Let's Talk is to be shared with other adults that are influential in a child's life: a spouse, ex-spouse, grandparent, daycare provider, teacher or neighbor.

Let's Connect has suggestions for parents and children, from infants to teens and everyone in-between.

> This week I had the chance to think about how I was raised: what I appreciated and what annoyed me.
>
> What do you remember about how you were raised?
>
> How are our past experiences influencing our parenting styles?
>
> In what ways do we complement each other?
>
> What challenges do we face?

It can be healthy for children to grow up in a family with a variety of personalities and interactions. No two parents or adults have to do things exactly the same way. Children accept, and enjoy, adults who are gentle and calm as well as those who are lively and energetic. If one parent is serious and a great listener, it is probably a healthy balance to have the other be more carefree and less intense.

Opportunities to evaluate parenting styles encourage adults to work together and make choices about the atmosphere they desire for their family. This on-going process builds trust and respect between adults. When adults agree to understand and support one another, children feel comfort and stability.

BUILD RELATIONSHIPS

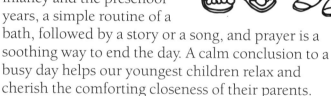

Evening Connections

Bedtime rituals and routines are memory makers for our children. During infancy and the preschool years, a simple routine of a bath, followed by a story or a song, and prayer is a soothing way to end the day. A calm conclusion to a busy day helps our youngest children relax and cherish the comforting closeness of their parents.

In the evening, elementary-aged children are often so busy with homework, soccer practice, piano lessons, and TV that parents hardly get to be with their kids at all. A 10-minute walk around the block, just for two, can be a time to bond with a child. For something extra special, try walking after dark, in the moonlight!

Are teenagers too big to be "tucked in?" Don't underestimate the importance of connecting with an older child at the end of the day. Just peeking in his/her room to drop off a glass of chocolate milk and say "good night" is a positive way to end the day and let our teens know we love them.

PRAYER REMINDERS

"For we are **God's workmanship,** created in Christ Jesus to do good works,
 which God prepared in **advance** for us to do."

—EPHESIANS 2:10

CHAPTER 2

MARTHA

VALUES Guide My Priorities

IN THIS SESSION

A Balancing Act

⮕ Raise your arm if you are a parent.

⮕ Raise your other arm if you are employed or volunteer outside the home.

⮕ Raise your leg if you have a parent or family member who depends on you.

⮕ Raise your other leg if you are involved in your church, community, or school.

⮕ Nod your head if this feels like a lot.

Look at what I need to get done today! >

MARTHA

*Luke 10:38—42;
John 11:17—12:3*

Martha, the sister of Mary and Lazarus, and close friend of Jesus, was a woman who knew how to get things done. In those days, it was the responsibility of the eldest sister to significantly contribute to help manage the home and family. She obviously learned to value hard work and didn't hesitate to be the one to jump up and serve the coffee and muffins or run down the road to greet a guest. We can imagine that she rarely sat still or put her feet up to rest. It seems that Martha's activity would have had her scurrying around from dawn to dusk.

At the death of her brother, Lazarus, we once again see Martha's dedication to take charge and attend to the details. She runs down the road to meet Jesus, rather than sitting patiently to wait for his arrival. When Jesus reaches the tomb of Lazarus and commands, "Take away the stone," Martha is thinking ahead to the implications of such an idea. "But, Lord," says Martha, "by this time there is a bad odor, for he has been there for four days." Martha, distracted by details, misses the "big picture," which is life in Jesus.

In pondering values and priorities, we see Martha as a character who was conditioned to be busy, at the expense of sacrificing relationships with people, especially Jesus.

Priorities are guided by our values. Search these verses to answer, *"What did Martha value?"*

Luke 10:38–42

John 11:20–22, 27, and 38–39

John 12:2

How did Martha view her purpose?

Does God have an additional purpose in mind for her? If so, what was it?

> *"Martha, Martha,"* the Lord answered, *"You are worried and upset about many things, but only one thing is needed."*
> LUKE 10:41–42

Jesus was speaking about "one thing" meaning spending time with him. We all need to be reminded that fussiness for things matters little, but time with Jesus matters much more.

How do we take time for prayer, meditation, reading, or perhaps a walk, just to focus on God?

Jesus replied: "Love the Lord your God with all your heart and with all your soul and with all your mind."

Matthew 22:37

TRIBUTE TO

Martha

Martha lived an organized life in a tidy home on the edge of a small town. She was ambitious and quick to respond to a need for service. Her friends remember her famous apple pie and perfect cup of coffee, but few can recall an uninterrupted conversation with this dear woman.

Martha's attention to details kept her from seeing the whole picture.
Look at the whole picture of our lives:

VALUES
PRIORITIES
PURPOSE

Imagine it is your 100th birthday! Picture yourself seated at a banquet, being held in your honor. Your hair is a beautiful shade of silver-gray. Your cane rests on the chair beside you. Your family, friends, neighbors, and business associates have all gathered to pay tribute to you and your life.

100th BIRTHDAY TRIBUTE TO

Insert my own name

What will they say?

What personal stories will they share about you?

What accomplishments will stand out?

Who will say you made a difference in their life?

DEFINING MY PURPOSE... WITH GOD'S HELP

"We need to get in the habit of standing back and looking at our lives and saying, 'Is this all? Is this all I want? Is something missing?' The biggest defect we humans have is our shortsightedness. **We don't see what we could be."**

—Morrie Schwartz,
Tuesdays With Morrie

WHAT DO I VALUE?

Reviewing my "Tribute" on the previous page, now make a list of the things I truly value.

WHAT FILLS MY DAYS?

*Fill in the spaces to record
activities during a normal day.*

6 am	
7 am	
8 am	
9 am	
10 am	
11 am	
noon	
1 pm	
2 pm	
3 pm	
4 pm	
5 pm	
6 pm	
7 pm	
8 pm	
9 pm	

*Is my time being spent on
the things I value most?*

Compare SCHEDULE with VALUES

Is my time being spent on the things I value most?
Scrutinize the schedule by asking:

What do I NEED to do?
What could I delegate to someone else?
What doesn't need to be done at all?

*Read one parent's reflections
after this experience:*

Tonight I had the opportunity to think through what I value and how I spend my days. I wrote that I value family, having fun with my kids, my career, and laughter. When I saw what fills my days, I was surprised to see how little of my time is spent in happy family times. Most of my time is spent in commuting, meetings, coaching kids' baseball, and rushing to grab a quick bite to eat.

So what will I do with this new insight? I'm not going to feel guilty and beat myself up about it. I'll just start today trying to live more what I value. In fact, tonight when I get home I plan to greet my family wearing a Bozo nose! It's about time we start laughing again!

MAKE IT HAPPEN!
**Write notes on the schedule
about changes I'd like to make.**

GIVING MY TIME

My time is a gift from God, but I just looked at my schedule and I don't have time to do one more thing!

What does God expect of my time?

- When the alarm goes off, hug my wife and tell her I love her.

- On a morning jog, greet neighbors with a smile.

- Help one of the kids find a lost homework paper, without lecturing.

- Take 5 minutes to really listen to my neighbor at the school bus stop.

- On the freeway, let someone cut in front.

- Wait 10 seconds to hold a door open for an elderly gentleman.

- Compliment a grocery bag boy on a job well done.

Did I change my schedule? If not, then what changed?

Karl, father of three boys, complained about never having time to get jobs done around the house because he was constantly interrupted. "My bike has a flat tire! Can we shoot hoops? Dad look at the worm I found! Can you read this to me? I'm really thirsty!"

After thinking about his values, Karl was able to see these interruptions as part of his priority to be a caring dad. With a change in his attitude, he now feels important to his sons, rather than dumped on!

WHAT IN MY LIFE COULD BECOME MEANINGFUL
WITH ONLY A CHANGE IN ATTITUDE?

PERSONAL TIME

I need some personal time to restore my energy!

COULD THESE OLD SAYINGS BE TRUE?

- ⭕ You can't get water from a dry well.
- ⭕ When I look good to myself, others look better to me.
- ⭕ We don't stop playing because we get old; we get old because we've stopped playing.

It appears that Martha found it hard to relax.

Is there any correlation between taking care of myself and my relationship with others?

What do I do just for FUN?

How does meeting my own needs benefit my family?

"I didn't know you won a medal for swimming. You never go swimming! I guess when you get to be a mother you don't care about having **fun** anymore."

—Beaver Cleaver,
to his mother, June

NO PERSONAL TIME?

Many parents feel trapped, especially when their children are very young, feeling that they have no opportunity to take time for themselves. One mom of three preschoolers said, "I'm all for taking care of myself, but I have NO personal time!"

BRAINSTORM SOME CREATIVE SOLUTIONS TO THIS PROBLEM:

Claudia has been up every night with her 3-week-old daughter. At first she found herself complaining about how tired and annoyed she was with the 2AM feeding time. She has now noticed how absolutely quiet her house is at 2 o'clock in the morning. Her older toddler, fast asleep, doesn't need her attention. There is no laundry buzzer calling to her. Her baby's coos are the only sounds that break the silence of the night. One night she pulled open the blinds and marveled at the moonlight streaming in her window. At other times she lights one candle for a soft glow in the room.

Claudia has grown to love her 2AM "personal time."

MAKE IT HAPPEN!
When can I schedule a personal time?

Don't just prioritize my schedule; schedule my priorities.

Getting to Know You

We humans need to preserve within ourselves a clearing, an inner space we keep exclusively for ourselves and God. A space for breathing, growing and listening that is nourished and fed.

A mother is often expected to look after others first and then, only if there's any time left over, "be herself." The trouble is that during the years of child-raising there is so little time left over. Work and free time are not so clearly defined for mothers. There is so much to do for others that taking time for ourselves comes low on the list of priorities.

I remember when, after a few years as the mother of young children, I went away for my first trip without them. I had lost the habit of being alone, of spending any time with myself. I was frightened. I felt insecure without all the familiar demands of others which had become my life. The individual, as opposed to the wife and mother, had grown weak from lack of practice.

We teach our children to be independent and self-reliant; to develop their own personalities—but do we follow our own lessons? For although children have a way of making us feel guilty if we take time from them, is it they who are making us feel guilty, or is it our own hesitation about taking time for ourselves? I think that deep down, especially as they grow older, children are worried and dismayed to feel that they are their mother's whole life. Nothing is heavier than the weight of another human being who is utterly dependent on us for fulfillment and happiness. It's good for children to learn that Mother values herself; that she has feelings and as-pirations that have nothing to do with them. That there is time that is hers alone, for her to do with as she likes.

So set aside time just for you. Be alone; think about your-self as a wonderful creation of God. Hold onto the dreams you had when there was no husband, no children. Because the day does come when life is not so full of the needs of oth-ers, when the children go away and the floor seems to stay clean all the time. Then you wake up and say, "Now that I have time, whatever happened to me?"

And you may find that the person you once were, or wanted to be, has left—gone somewhere, disappeared, and that there is nobody left where she once lived.

Find her before she leaves. Give her space to breathe and grow. Remember that she's absolutely unique with valuable ideas and skills that can glorify her Creator.

> **"My business is not to remake myself, but to make the absolute best of what God has made."**
> **—Robert Browning**

VALUES Guide my PRIORITIES

There is a time for everything...
A time to weep and a time to laugh,
A time to mourn and a time to dance,
A time to embrace and a time to refrain,
A time to be silent and a time to speak.

—ECCLESIASTES 3:1–7

"Seek true success in people, relationships, faith, love, and service. Measure success in lives saved, minds taught, people served, and love given."

—Kevin W. McCarthy,
The On-Purpose Person

REFLECTIONS

Today I considered my values, schedule, personal time, and time with God. One small thing I can do to find balance in my life is...

IMPACT MY FAMILY

Let's Talk

This week I had the chance to think about my priorities and how I spend my time.

As a parent, often my child is the priority. However, an adult relationship is essential to building a strong family. What can we do to prioritize our relationship and devote time to being alone, without children?

It is easy to focus priorities on what we wish we could do for our children. However, in a child-centered world, our marriages rarely get the priority they need.

Many families have resolved themselves to the "fact" that during the child-rearing years a marriage has to come second to the needs of the children. True, there are emergencies and situations where we ought to drop everything and tend to our children. But this easily becomes the norm, and that is not healthy.

Protect adult time with:

15 minute "coffee talk" after dinner. Depending on the age of the children, ask children to do kitchen clean up while mom and dad take their coffee into the living room for 15 minutes of uninterrupted time to talk about the day. Even very young children can learn that this is a special time for them to play quietly alone.

Earlier bedtimes. Consider earlier bedtimes to give parents some time alone. As children get older and their time to fall asleep is later than their parents' they can respect a time, say 9PM, when parents are off-limits. Any signatures or questions can be handled before 9 o'clock, because after that parents will be relaxing together, or apart, but not attending to the demands of children.

Couple time brings strength to a marriage and family. To a great extent, children are more secure when they feel the endurance of a quality marriage. Likewise, for single parents, preserving some time without children, perhaps for conversation with another supportive adult, is imperative to balance and happiness.

BUILD RELATIONSHIPS

Let's Connect

Quality Time

Rocking the baby or falling asleep on the sofa with a toddler are not wasted time. The comfort and safe feeling of relaxing together builds a special bond.

Try to start school days out with a smile. Share a laugh, a quip, or perhaps a childhood story. A positive morning exchange lingers throughout the day, a memory for both child and parent to share.

Just because teenagers are old enough to come home after school to an empty house doesn't mean they like it. Everyone feels better when met with a warm greeting. Adjusting schedules, when possible, shows teens parents value them. Try giving a phone call, leaving cookies on the counter, or writing a welcome home note for teens coming home alone.

PRAYER REMINDERS

Jesus replied: "Love the Lord your God
with all your heart and with all your soul
and with all your mind."

—MATTHEW 22:37

THOMAS

My child is UNIQUE

IN THIS SESSION

Which am I?

- A morning person…or…a night-owl?
- Hot tea…or…an ice cold coke?
- Warm summer…or…cool winter colors?
- Sensible…or…imaginative?

God sure made me different from you!

THOMAS

*John 11:11–16
and 20:24–31*

Thomas is one of the disciples who stands out from the group of Jesus' twelve chosen followers as being unique. Sometimes we think of Thomas as a flawed character, "doubting Thomas," but in actuality it is probably just his unique personality that is evident.

In John 11, Jesus is going to Lazarus, who has already died. Thomas, in his intense love for Jesus, is so eager to be a supportive part of Jesus' work that he suggests, "Let us also go, that we may die with him." What an extreme reaction! That seems to be Thomas' style.

After the crucifixion, Thomas is unable to believe his friends when they tell him that Jesus is alive. This is not a defect in his character, but another illustration of his unique, intense temperament. Perhaps the image of the crucifixion had filled his mind so completely that he was unable to be comforted by words alone. He needed more proof.

Jesus understood Thomas and knew how to lovingly grant him the means he needed to be satisfied. Jesus modeled for us how to accept and understand individual personalities; He accepts all of us with our strengths and weaknesses.

Read John 20:24–31
What do these verses tell us about Thomas' personality?

How did Jesus respond to Thomas' uniqueness?

What does Jesus' reaction to Thomas teach us about relating to other people?

▼ ▼

"For you created my inmost being;
you knit me together in my mother's womb.
I praise you because I am fearfully and wonderfully made;
your works are wonderful,
I know that full well.
My frame was not hidden from you
when I was made in the secret place.
When I was woven together in the depths of the earth,
your eyes saw my unformed body.
All the days ordained for me
were written in your book
before one of them
came to be."

—Psalm 139:13–16

▲ ▲

How do these verses make me feel about myself?

God created me to be one-of-a-kind!

What things are especially difficult for me?

What things are easier for me than for most people?

God knows me and understands me,
with all my strengths and weaknesses,
He comes to me in a way I will be able to see Him,
unlike the way He comes to any other person.
He knows I am unique,
and He uses my uniqueness to bring me closer to Him.

Children come to us like a packet of flower seeds, with no pictures on the cover, and no guarantees. We do not know what they will look like, be like, or act like. Our job, like the gardener's, is to meet their specific needs as best we can, uncovering their innate potential to turn into a grown plant. Remember that all plants are different, needing varying amounts of care and attention. A parent who understands individual differences is able to nourish a child, just as water and sun nourish a plant.

"fearfully and wonderfully made..."

I UNDERSTAND THAT MY CHILD IS UNIQUE!

A QUICK TEMPERAMENT QUIZ

ADAPTABILITY
How quickly does my child adapt to new foods? New places? Changes in schedule? Changes in routine? Surprises?

1 (quickly)　　　2　　3　　4　　5 (slowly)

FIRST REACTION
How does my child usually react when meeting new people for the first time? Doing a new activity? Going somewhere new?

1 (jumps in)　　　2　　3　　4　　5 (rejection or watches)

INTENSITY OF REACTION
How strong is my child's reaction? Laugh or cry loudly and energetically? Or softly and mildly?

1 (mild)　　　2　　3　　4　　5 (intense)

REGULARITY
Is my child regular about eating times? Sleeping times? Amount of sleep needed?

1 (regular)　　　2　　3　　4　　5 (irregular)

SENSITIVITY
How aware is my child of slight noises? Slight differences in temperature? Tastes? Textures in clothing?

1 (not sensitive)　　2　　3　　4　　5 (very sensitive)

GENERAL MOOD
How much of the time does my child feel pleasant, happy, contented compared with serious, analytical, or discontented?

1 (positive)　　　2　　3　　4　　5 (more serious)

SCORES:		
6–12 Cool	13–19 Spunky	20–30 Spirited

For more information see Kurchinka, *Raising Your Spirited Child*; or Chess, Thomas & Birch, *Your Child is a Person.*

Is my Child SPIRITED? SPUNKY? or COOL?

How do I feel about that?

This scale represents a child's natural way of reacting, also called "temperament." Every person has a unique temperament, meaning that we all perceive the world a bit differently.

Temperament scores are not good or bad; right or wrong. However, this information can help parents consider their child's unique tendencies and predict a child's reactions. With this knowledge and foresight, parents can be more understanding and more effective.

A+

Temperaments are not GOOD or BAD

People have one thing in common; they are all different.

One parent recalls...

My son is "spirited." At first I wondered what I had done wrong to make him turn out so strong-willed! Then I realized this is the unique way God created him.

As a young boy he was so persistent! If he was in the middle of creating an intricate spaceship or airplane, it was impossible to convince him to stop for dinner. I learned that he needed to be notified at least 10 minutes before dinner, so he could begin to break away from his activity.

Now that he's older, it's easier to see the positives of his intensity. He still has many of the same characteristics, but they work to his benefit! For example, his energy level surpasses that of most of his colleagues, and he is determined to excel with every project.

It was not my job to "break" his strong will, but to understand his natural reaction to things. With calm coaching he was able to learn appropriate ways to manage himself and still keep his "spirit."

And another parent said...

People say I'm lucky that Molly is so "calm," but it bothers me when they call her "shy." Now that I know it is hard for her to meet new people and try new things, I've been able to think of some creative ways to help her.

For example, when we're driving to a play date, I talk with Molly about what she can expect when we get there. That seems to help her prepare herself and feel more at ease. We also brainstorm things she can say to join into the group. Practicing some specific phrases she can use, like, "Do you want to use my shovel to dig in the sand?" or "I think you are very good at climbing," is teaching Molly how to join in.

How can this information help a parent?

When parents understand the tendencies of their children they are able to respond in ways that can calm intense children, comfort sensitive ones, and encourage the cautious.

Predict child responses to the situation below, then brainstorm parenting strategies for each.

	Age 14, getting ready for the first day of High School	What could a parent do to be sensitive and effective?
How will a spirited child respond?		
How will a spunky child respond?		
How will a cool child respond?		

What about My child?

Write a few sentences to describe what I've realized about my child and his/her unique temperament.

Use the temperament quiz (page 47) to get started thinking

Is there one aspect of my child's temperament that seems to be causing him/her some challenges these days?

How can I be most helpful as he/she meets these challenges?

Understanding my child
influences my response.

MY CHILD IS A UNIQUE INDIVIDUAL

We are "fearfully and wonderfully" created by God to be different from every other person on earth. It is our responsibility as parents to understand what makes each of our children unique: their strengths and their challenges. With that understanding, I can help my child blossom into the person God has intended him, or her, to be.

REFLECTIONS

After thinking about my child's unique challenges and how I can be helpful, what will I need to be most effective?

What will I do?

IMPACT MY FAMILY

Let's Talk

This week I thought about children as unique individuals, each with their own distinct temperament.

Look at my responses to the temperament quiz on page 47. Does this seem like an accurate picture of my child?

Take an opportunity to ask another adult to review your perception of your child. Sometimes we think we know our children but, being so close to them, it's easy to become blind to things that may be clear to others.

What about my temperament? Examining our own tendencies can enable us to trace our reactions back to a specific aspect of our temperament. To be an effective parent, knowing myself is as important as understanding my child.

BUILD RELATIONSHIPS

Celebrate Uniqueness

Let's Connect

Create an "I Am Special" booklet for, or with, young children. Babies love to look at close up photos of faces. Include photos of them and other familiar people on the pages of a homemade book. Encourage young children to scribble with markers or crayons to make personalized pages. Then, "read" this book together, over and over again, telling about the characteristics that make the child unlike any other child in the world.

Bring out some old family photo albums that depict children "way back" when they were babies. Tell the stories that go along with the photos: the day he was born; the time she dumped her macaroni on top of her head; how he loved to sing a special song in the bathtub. All these stories tell children that they are "one-of-a-kind" kids and they are precious to us.

At a time when a teen is home, pop in an old family video of him as an adorable little kid. Notice how he could dance even as a preschooler, or loved to climb, or enjoyed soft things. Watch for little gestures or habits that are still part of the teen's character today. Let him know how much his parents enjoyed his childhood, and still enjoy his company today.

PRAYER REMINDERS

"I praise God because I am fearfully and wonderfully made;

His works are wonderful."

—PSALMS 139:14

.

PETER

MISTAKES are Opportunities to Learn

How do I feel about mistakes?

We're making progress if today's mistakes are different from yesterday's.

Making a mistake does NOT equal being a mistake.

Mistakes are a detour, not a dead end street.

I have not made 10,000 mistakes. I have successfully found 10,000 ways that will not work.

PETER

Matthew Chapters 4, 14, 16, 17, 26; Acts

Peter was a fisherman, originally named Simon, whom Jesus chose to be one of his followers. An impulsive personality, Peter was prone to making mistakes. Several of Peter's blunders are recorded throughout the gospel books of Matthew, Mark, Luke, and John. He speaks without thinking, acts impulsively, and breaks promises. He sounds like any one of us!

However, as we continue to read about his life, we see that he obviously learned from his mistakes. He goes on to become a recognized leader among Jesus' disciples, one of the inner group of three. Jesus renamed him "Peter" because it means "rock," and Jesus promised that "on this rock I will build my church." Matthew 16:18. It was through Peter's mistakes that he learned valuable lessons to prepare him for the important work that was ahead. The book of Acts begins with an account of Peter's work to establish and grow the church in Jerusalem.

Jesus wasn't looking for a perfect person when he selected Peter, and he isn't looking for perfection in us or in our children. Jesus expects us to make mistakes, plenty of them, and then use those mistakes to learn what we need to lead our lives for him.

In each of these passages, "What was Peter's mistake?"

Matthew 14:22−33

Matthew 16:21−23

Matthew 26:31−35 and 26: 69−75

Matthew 26:36−46

PETER'S LIFE-CHANGING MISTAKES

Why do I think Peter acted the way he did? Why did he make the mistake he made?

Matthew 14:22–33

Matthew 16:21–23

Matthew 26:31–35 and 26: 69–75

Matthew 26:36–46

- Peter attempted, unsuccessfully, to walk on water but learned the importance of trusting God.

- He disagreed with God's plan for Jesus' life, but through that he learned to accept God's will.

- He made the mistake of denying Jesus but, out of his grief, learned to stand up for Jesus with new conviction.

- When Jesus was in the garden to pray, Peter fell asleep, but learned to acknowledge his human weaknesses.

Peter made mistakes but through those errors he was transformed into a man of strong character, fit to do the work God had in mind for him.

Mistakes can be
opportunities to learn.

Do I feel comfortable with mistakes?

Take an
ATTITUDE CHECK!

WHAT'S A PARENT TO DO ABOUT MISTAKES?

IT'S A PARENT'S ROLE TO:

Take on an attitude that says, "Mistakes are opportunities to learn"

Stop and understand WHY our children's mistakes have occurred

Forgive our children and move forward

Parents generally have a tough time allowing children to experience mistakes. When our kids make mistakes, we feel inadequate. When we aren't able to control our child's behavior, we panic. If there is another adult within earshot, we are concerned about what they think of us as parents.

Mistakes help kids learn skills they need for life: problem solving, negotiation, and resourcefulness. Let kids make mistakes! They will grow through opportunities to face a challenge, attempt a solution, sometimes feel failure, but eventually experience the satisfaction of a problem solved.

MISTAKES...

My toddler tripped and fell down on the living room floor, but that's OK; he's just learning to walk.

MISTAKES...

Of course my first grader mispro-nounces a word now and then; he's only learning to read.

MISTAKES...

Some of our children's mistakes are pretty easy to accept. We know that they are learning new skills and we expect them to make mistakes.

But how about...

- A two year old throwing a temper tantrum? Am I able to say that she's learning to express her feelings?

- A teenager missing curfew time? Am I able to say that she's in the process of learning responsibility?

What good things can come from mistakes?

Are mistakes REALLY opportunities to learn?

What mistakes have we made lately? >

What are we still learning that < *would cause us to make such mistakes?*

With knowledge about the normal learning that occurs at each stage of our child's development, we are better able to understand their mistakes.

WHy?

TODDLERS ARE LEARNING

Toddlers and young preschoolers are learning to manage their bodies and their environment. It is NORMAL for them to:

- Move a lot! Run, jump, and climb on everything, but not necessarily with balance or control.
- Express their new found opinions with "NO!" or tantrums.
- Have short attention spans as they are easily distracted by so many interesting things.
- Show interest in other children, but not in sharing
- Exert independence with "do it myself!"
- Be egocentric with "Me first!"

WHy?

If I understand **WHY** my child makes mistakes, I can make better parenting decisions.

SCHOOL-AGE TENDENCIES

In elementary school a child's world expands beyond home and family
It is NORMAL for them to:

- Think in black and white, with no gray areas. Things are right or wrong, and it is hard to help this child see possible exceptions.

- Still learn best through trial and error. Lectures don't change a kid's mind; kids need to see things for themselves.

- Have lots of ideas, but no forethought to see the consequences.

- Invent projects and create plans, but not be organized enough to see them through to completion.

- Learn to take responsibility.

WHY?

TASK OF TEENS

During the teen years, our kids are striving to become self-reliant, independent, and individual.
It is NORMAL for teens to:

WHY?

- Spend lots of time with friends.
- Desire independence and freedom.
- Disagree with parents as they practice independence.
- Feel invincible.
- Experience intense emotions and mood swings.
- Waiver between confidence and insecurity.
- Need some privacy.
- Still want affection and care from parents, even though it's sometimes hard for them to ask.

DON'T FIX IT!

Do I see mistakes as a challenge for parents to **FIX?** Or a learning experience for a child?

See how two parents try to fix Carly's problem:

Carly: *I'm leaving now, Mom! Bye!*
Mom: *What about that Spanish test you have tomorrow?*
C: *Oh, it's too late to worry about that. I'll never have time to learn everything I need to know in just one night.*
M: *I could quiz you.*
C: *No, I need to meet Brian at the mall.*
M: *Why don't you at least read the summary? Here's the page.*
C: *That doesn't help much.*
M: *While you do your hair, just listen and I'll read it to you.*
C: *If you want to...*
M: *OK, we can learn this.*
C: *You are way more worried about this than I am!*

Carly: *I'm leaving now, Dad! Bye!*
Dad: *What about that Spanish test you have tomorrow?*
C: *Oh, it's too late to worry about that. I'll never have time to learn everything I need to know in just one night.*
D: *Going out when you have studying to do is not an option.*
C: *I need to meet Brian at the mall.*
D: *I said, "No."*
C: *But I have to go! Brian is waiting for me.*
D: *Your grades are much more important to me than having you see Brian.*
C: *You are so unfair! I hate you!*
D: *You're grounded!*

What was Carly's mistake?
What did she learn from each situation?
What might she have learned if her parents hadn't jumped in to "fix it?"

Giving teens control of their own study schedules provides the opportunity for them to make wise decisions, or perhaps make mistakes and be unprepared for that test. For a teen who is working to develop independence and responsibility, the power to make this decision will provide a valuable life lesson, more important than any Spanish content.

SHOW UNDERSTANDING
LISTEN
ASK GOOD QUESTIONS

Hold yourself back! Don't jump in to fix kid's problems! Put your FIX–IT toolbox away and instead:

• Show understanding. Make comments to help define the problem and show empathy.
• Listen and be there. A physical presence shows support and helps young children stay focused.
• Ask good questions to help a child clarify the problem in his own mind. A question can sometimes help a child see an issue in a different light.

See what happens when a parent allows Carly to fix her own problem:

Carly: *I'm leaving now! Bye!*
Parent: *What about that Spanish test you have tomorrow?*
C: *Oh, it's too late to worry about that. I'll never have time to learn everything I need to know in just one night.*
P: *Sounds like you have a LOT to study. (UNDERSTANDING)*
C: *Yeah, it's huge and I need to meet Brian at the mall.*
P: *So this a big dilemma. You have plans with Brian and you have a lot to learn for Spanish. (UNDERSTANDING)*
C: *I already told you it's too late for that test.*
P: *Really? (LISTENING)*
C: *Yes, I'm going to take whatever grade I get, and see Brian tonight.*
P: *Hmmm. (LISTENING)*
C: *C'mon, I'm not going to flunk Spanish. I know what I have to do to pass this class.*
P: *If you get a low grade on this test, what are your options? (QUESTION)*
C: *Here's what I've been thinking...*

Parents don't help children by insulating them from the stuff of real life. Kids are strengthened by facing challenges, and empowered with the sense of accomplishment that comes from solving their own problems.

You spilled your milk? I warned you to be more careful! You should have asked for my help! No more milk for you!

FORGIVE CHILDREN

Whoops! What do you need to do to clean up? I know yo can fix it!

Once a mistake has been made, it's so tempting to make kids "feel the pain" of their error. Our anger and frustration is understandable, but not helpful. It does no good to linger over "spilled milk" and make our kids feel worse. Parents who react in anger can inadvertently put up a wall between themselves and their children, causing kids to lie or hide mistakes in the future.

What we ought to do is calmly encourage kids to fix their own mistakes and show them, through our love and forgiveness, that we are the ones they can come to when mistakes are made. When your kids make a mistake, whatever it is, remember spilled milk, forgive it and work together to make a plan for "clean up."

> **"Where did we ever get the crazy idea that in order to make kids do better we must first make them feel worse?**
>
> **—Jane Nelson,**
> author *Positive Discipline*

ASK TO BE FORGIVEN

I remember one evening after a very hard day of work when I was especially grouchy with my ten-year-old daughter. After getting into bed that night, I knew I hadn't treated her right, and I needed to ask for her forgiveness.

Before she left for school the next morning, I said, with sweaty palms and a lump in my throat, "Honey, I know that you realize parents aren't perfect, and I'm sorry I was not fair with you last night."

She put her arms around my neck and said, "Dad, it's alright." She was so forgiving! Asking my daughter to forgive me showed her, and me, that I have flaws like anyone else. Kids aren't the only ones who make mistakes in my house. Saying "I'm sorry" sets an example for my children to admit their mistakes, rather than hide them, and to feel confident that they will be forgiven.

Many people have a hard time saying they are sorry to anyone, let alone their children. Take time to consider your own personal experiences and feelings about forgiveness by writing an acrostic poem.

F

O

R

G

I

V

E

"Forgive as the Lord forgave you."

Colossians 3:13

69

LEARNING for LIFE

As a father of three, any problem in our house was a challenge for me to solve. When my younger children got into an argument, I simply sent both of them to their rooms. When my teenager questioned my authority, he was grounded. If someone complained about a meal, they got no dinner that night. In my house problems were really no problem—I knew how to take care of them!

One day at work I heard other parents, whose children were older, complain that their college-aged kids couldn't make decisions, and their young adult children couldn't get along with co-workers. I got an uneasy feeling as I began to question whether what I was doing was really the best for my children. I got to wondering if the way I was raising my children, constantly controlling them, was actually teaching them not to value their own ideas. By telling them the correct way—MY WAY—of doing things, was I teaching them to doubt themselves, to look to me rather than to themselves for approval? I realized that, in truth, I valued compliance more than cooperation.

I was inspired to make a change but didn't know how to get started. I wanted to give my children more responsibility and fewer rules, but I worried about what other people would think when they saw me allowing, no – expecting, my children to direct at least some of their own behaviors. And I had moments of doubt: Could children really learn this way? If I didn't tell them what to do, would they really figure it out?

The potential benefits seemed to be worth the risk, so I decided to give it a shot. I started by listening, rather than instructing. I forced myself to pause and observe, rather than jumping to offer solutions. I watched my children think for themselves and make decisions that were occasionally the same decision I would have made, but many times were different. Plenty of mistakes were made, but at least my children were still living in the safety of our home. In a few short years, my children would be young adults living far away from the support of a family.

Over time, I have watched my children become more competent, confident people, with skill in tactfully defending their opinions and standing up for what they believe. They shine with the good feelings that come from a sense of accomplishment. I know that with this new style of parenting I am encouraging my children to think creatively, to act independently, and to follow their own paths. In my opinion, instilling these values is worth the extra effort.

It wasn't without agony and adjustment, but I can honestly say that it was one parenting decision where I think I "got it right." What have I learned? I learned that children who are encouraged to think learn more than those who are made to live what someone else has already thought. I learned that parents do have a role of providing learning opportunities, observing, supporting and guiding their children. But the learning is theirs. And mistakes are a pretty good teacher.

MISTAKES ARE OPPORTUNITIES TO LEARN

Mistakes happen to all of us. Our children need to know that we do not expect perfection but we see mistakes as opportunities to learn. With an atti-tude of acceptance, love, and forgiveness, our children learn to trust us and confide in us, knowing that we will support them as they learn to fix their own mistakes and encourage them to do better next time.

REFLECTIONS

How do I normally react when my child makes a mistake? What is one thing I would like to remember this week?

IMPACT MY FAMILY

Let's
Talk

Today I had the time to consider how I react when my
child makes mistakes.

What mistakes do you see
children making that are
challenging for you to accept?
How can we support one
another in the issues that
"push our buttons."

Some mistakes are more difficult than others for parents
to handle calmly. Everyone has pet issues that irritate them.
When faced with these "hot buttons" it is helpful to have
another caring adult for discussion and support.

With a spouse or
friend, decide how you
can help each other
understand the "WHY"
of your child's mistakes,
as well as brainstorm
ways to be effective
without charging in
to fix the problem for
your child.

BUILD RELATIONSHIPS

Let's Connect

Share Successes

Make up songs with your baby or toddler, using her name, to acknowledge accomplishments and skills she has gained. For example, to the tune of "Are You Sleeping?" you might sing, "Anna is climbing, Anna is climbing, Yes she is! Anna can climb, Anna can climb. Yes she can. Yes she can." Hearing her name and getting your undivided attention lets her know that she is a special person.

Some families have purchased a "special plate" to be used at dinner for a family member who has accomplished something that day. The plate, perhaps bright red or a fun yellow, is brought out and placed at the dinner table place for someone who did especially well on a math test, or someone who was particularly kind to a neighbor, or whatever your family decides to recognize.

Make a "big deal" of your teen's accomplishments. Be creative and present your son with a plastic football award if he will be starting in Friday night's game. When finals are over, bring out your daughter's favorite ice cream bars for the whole family, in celebration of her hard work all week. Teens will probably act embarrassed, but they'll remember these little things forever, and feel loved.

PRAYER REMINDERS

"Forgive
as the Lord forgave you."
—COLOSSIANS 3:13

PAUL

Encourage SUCCESS

✓ **Consider** success as a life de-pendent on God.

Encourage My Children?

I always do! But one night while entertaining guests, Ted and Evelyn, I wondered what would happen if I spoke to my guests the same way I speak to my children...

✓ **Develop skills that set my child up for success:**

- *understanding what to expect*
- *saying what I understand*

"Well, it's about time you two got here! You are 15 minutes late. You are such dawdlers. Leave those muddy shoes at the door. Were you born in a barn?"

"So, Evelyn, how have you been? I've been meaning to have you over for such a long time. Hey, Ted, take it easy on that chip dip or you'll ruin your appetite. I haven't been cooking all afternoon for you to pick at your meal like a bird. Here let me move it away from you."

"Have you heard from the gang lately? Yes, the Olson's are in Florida for the winter. Evelyn, did you wash your face before you came? Here let me get this spot around your mouth. Oh, I guess it's a shadow."

"Well, let's eat. Ted, I only poured you a half cup of coffee. You know how clumsy you can be. Evelyn, don't talk with your mouth full. I can't understand a word you're saying."

At that moment in my fantasy my son walked in the room. "How nice to see you," I said pleasantly. "Now what did I do?" he sighed.

Adapted from a piece by the late Erma Bombeck

PAUL

Paul was an apostle used by God to make missionary journeys to share the Good News of Jesus. Early in his life Paul persecuted Christians, but God dramatically changed him so he would be able to teach and encourage Christians in the early church.

Paul carried the gospel to people in cities who had never before heard it, and he wrote letters to people in those same cities: Rome, Corinth, Galatia, Ephesus, Philippi, Colosse, Thessalonica. He was a traveler, teaching the gospel and encouraging many people in their faith.

Parents do not need to travel around the world to encourage others in their faith. We have important work to do in our own homes, influencing our children as they are discovering their own understanding and relationship with Jesus. Paul's writings provide us with valuable messages for our lives today—messages we can share with our children.

From these verses...	What would Paul say "success" is?	What do I think of Paul's encouraging advice?
Phil 1:3–11		
Phil 2:1–4 Phil 4:4–9		
1 Tim 6:11–16		

▼ ▼

"Therefore encourage one another and build each other up, just as in fact you are doing."
—I Thessalonians 5:11

Are there people in my life who encourage me in my faith? What do they do?

How do I encourage my children in their faith?

▲ ▲

PAUL'S LESSON FOR PARENTS

Paul's source of wisdom was God. When Paul traveled into new cities, he was delivering God's message, but he knew the Spirit of God was at work through him. I am encouraged that the Spirit of God is working through me to rear my children when I allow Him to be the source of my wisdom. Paul was relying on God, and I need to also. My children are God's work in progress. I will lay them in His hands

The **Spirit of God** is **working** through me to rear my children.

GROWING IN FAITH
How do parents encourage children to grow in faith?

You thought I wasn't listening!

I learned what you believe

I heard you say a prayer, and I learned there is a God I can always talk to and trust.

I saw you make a meal and take it to a friend who was sick, and I learned that we all have to help take care of each other.

I saw you give of your time and money to help people who had nothing, and I learned that those who have something should give to those who don't.

I saw you invite Christian friends into my life, and I learned to value relationships with people who care about me.

I felt you listen to me when I questioned who God was, and I learned to discover God's love.

All these things I learned because you lived what you believe.

BUILDING SUCCESS
How do parents encourage children to be successful?

UNDERSTANDING WHAT TO EXPECT

Understanding what to expect at each stage helps me accept my child's challenges and encourage his development.

Since toddlers are just developing the ability to manipulate small, intricate things, like buttons on a shirt, I won't expect him to hurry getting dressed. That would be like me trying to button a shirt while wearing a pair of mittens!

SAYING WHAT I UNDERSTAND

When my child is struggling to get dressed I might say, "I know it's tough for your small fingers to get a button through that tiny hole. You can do it! I'll wait and watch."

SET CHILDREN UP FOR SUCCESS!

success (sek-ses'), n., 1. helping children become independent of parents, and dependent on God.

SUCCESS AT EACH AGE
Understand What to Expect

Get Inside the Mind of a Toddler

My toddler climbs on everything. Instead of watching TV sitting still on a chair, he is balancing on the arm of the sofa or draped over a stack of pillows he pulled off every piece of furniture we own. He loves to jump off things, and he isn't very balanced or coordinated, so that worries me, too. He is so physical!

I have tried explaining to him that he could get hurt if he falls, but he doesn't seem to be able to stop stretching those muscles of his. I know that these muscles are growing really fast inside his little body. It seems that everything he wants to do is active. He loves to ride his tricycle and play at the playground, so I try to get him outdoors as much as I can.

When I make an issue of keeping the living room neat and don't allow him to climb on the furniture, he gets so angry with me. He shouts, "NO!" (his favorite word these days), and even hits me. I wish he would learn to tell me with words what he is thinking. I think he is even physical in his communication! I need to figure out how to keep him safe, and still let him work on being a toddler!

What do I understand about toddlers and this situation?

How can I encourage my toddler?

What's realistic for my age?

Which of these statements show a parent's attitude that would "set an infant or toddler up for success?"

INFANTS AND TODDLERS

☐ Hannah never puts objects in her mouth.

☐ We stopped going to that play-group because those toddlers hit.

☐ In church I expect Hannah to sit nice and still.

☐ Hannah waits patiently

☐ I let Hannah look at my special books because I know she won't rip them.

☐ My schedule has become more flexible now that I have an infant.

☐ Hannah sometimes cries when I leave the room.

Get Inside the Mind of a Toddler

My preschool daughter has a great imagination. She can play dress-up, or school, or grocery store for hours. But lately her imagination is causing problems at bedtime.

She dreams up imaginary green-eyed monsters and creatures that she thinks will come popping out of her closet or climb in through her window. Her fears are so vivid that she has trouble falling asleep, and often has bad dreams. I try to talk with her but the things she's afraid of are so irrational that it's hard for me to understand her thinking. I tell her these creatures are not real, but she doesn't believe me.

My mother-in-law says these fears are the result of watching too much TV. My neighbor thinks it's due to all her pretending; she has trouble remembering which things are real and which are pretend. My father says I should get tough with her and tell her to "snap out of it."

I know that this is a phase which needs my support. I also know that her thinking is not like that of an adult so telling her to not worry, or telling her to "snap out of it" is useless. That would show her that I am not understanding or accepting how she feels. Even though I do not understand her fears, I can tell her that I understand that she is feeling upset. Together we can work on ways she can take control of her fears. I want her to know that I will be here to encourage her.

What do I understand about preschoolers and this situation?

How can I encourage my preschooler?

What's realistic for my age?

Which of these statements show a parent's attitude that would "set a preschooler up for success?"

PRESCHOOLERS

☐ Sammy puts the napkins on the table for dinner.

☐ I expect Sam to always share his toys.

☐ I tell Sammy, "There's no reason to cry".

☐ When the little neighbor boy comes to play, some-times the boys argue.

☐ Sammy is generally fine when I leave him at preschool, but sometimes he cries.

☐ Sam loves to skip and hop, but still occasionally falls.

Understanding Life as a School-Age Child

I'm so glad that my son still enjoys spending time with me and is proud to call me his parent. I am delighted that he is so eager to help me with chores, both inside and outside the house. So, what's my concern? His mind never shuts down!

Whether we are working together, eating a meal, or driving in the car, my son is always thinking. He seems to have so many things on his mind these days. He wants to tell me every detail about his social studies project, last night's episode of his favorite TV show, and that last play in Saturday's football game. All this detail just wears me out. He plans a big project, calls three friends, and wants me to bake cookies, all in the same hour!

I know that during these years, his brain is soaking up volumes of new information. I need to remember that he doesn't have the mature capabilities he needs to prioritize all this data he's taking in. I can help him understand how to process his new ideas and learn organizational skills. I also need to set aside some time for undivided attention, where I am sincerely interested in his ideas, asking questions and searching with him to find out more about things he's interested in.

What do I understand about school-age children and this situation?

How can I encourage my school-age child?

What's realistic for my age?

Which of these statements show a parent's attitude that would "set a school-age child up for success?"

SCHOOL-AGE CHILDREN

☐ Nick can clean up his own messes.

☐ At dinner we are constantly telling Nick that he talks too much.

☐ Nick is old enough to pour milk without ever spilling.

☐ I want Nick to be friends with Aaron, the smartest boy in the class.

☐ I know that organization is a difficult thing for kids this age to learn.

☐ Nick's school project was a great idea, but it didn't work out perfectly.

☐ I want Nick to look good so I choose his school outfits for him.

Take a Teenager's Perspective

My teen insists on playing his music at top volume. I realize that from his perspective, loud music feels fun, party-like… Hey, IT REALLY ROCKS! When his friends are around loud music makes him feel "cool" and accepted. Low volume just doesn't have the same effect. And the songs (if you can call them songs) he chooses! He keeps telling me that he is becoming different from me. Well, we certainly have different tastes in music!

I understand his perspective, but I can't agree with it…(the neighbors are calling about the music, I have a headache, and those "big-buck" speakers could blow at any minute.) It helps me to remember that my teen is still a child. He is growing bigger and smarter, but he is still a child. I can't expect him to think like an adult. He hasn't thought of all the boring reasons to turn down the music. (Luckily, he has me, and I am pretty good at thinking of these reasons!)

I must get the music turned softer. However, with my understanding of his perspective, I will try not to be angry but will remember that he is doing what is right in his mind.

I will address the issue by letting him know that I do understand how he feels, that I've thought about his perspective, and that the doors to communication are open. I will tell him my concerns without shaming, blaming, or causing a power struggle.

> *What do I understand about teenagers and this situation?*
>
>
> *How can I encourage my teen?*

What's realistic for my age?

Which of these statements show a parent's attitude that would "set a teenager up for success?"

TEENAGERS

☐ I expect Monica to schedule time for a family dinner at least once a week.

☐ I will not stand for Monica disagreeing with me.

☐ Some days Monica is quiet and moody.

☐ Monica cares too much about being with her friends.

☐ There are some issues we disagree on.

☐ When I say, "Because I said so!" Monica understands.

☐ I know Monica is practicing to be independent.

☐ Monica is old enough to not make mistakes.

*ALSO REMEMBER TEMPERAMENT:

At any age, our individual child's unique personality influences our expectations.

SHOW UNDERSTANDING
Say What I Understand

There is nearly always a reason for children's behaviors. Take their perspective, understand where they are in their development, and try to understand their reasoning. Even if I don't understand everything, I can let children know what I do understand; what I observe. My statements can provide clarity to a child who often doesn't understand himself.

Wow, something's really got you upset.

It seems to me that you think...

You sound...

It sounds to me like you are feeling...

That must have been...

TELL WHAT I DO UNDERSTAND!
Understanding is not the same as agreeing.

What do I understand about this situation? Why does my child care so much?

The sample "starters" on the previous page help parents respond with comments that show understanding.

It takes time to feel comfortable speaking this way, with comments that express our understanding without attempting to fix the problem. However, it is worth our time and practice to help our children clarify their own thinking.

"Carrie is having a huge birthday party, and I am the only one not invited. I hate her!"

"That must have been a disappointment."

"This big kid is bugging me at lunch. He steps in front of me in line and knocks my tray. Today I nearly dropped my whole tray on the floor."

"Wow! That's really upsetting to be picked on."

"This new haircut is so ugly I will not go to school!"

"It sounds like you are feeling embarrassed and afraid of what the kids will say."

Just knowing that my mom and dad understand how I feel makes problems easier to handle.

Recall a challenging situation my child is facing. Write a comment that shows understanding.

"The purpose of parenting is to see with the eyes of another, feel with the heart of another, and walk in the shoes of another."

—ALFRED ADLER

93

ENCOURAGE SUCCESS

The world defines success in ways that we may not agree are best for our children. It is the role of a parent to stay in tune with "what is normal" for their children as they grow—holding high expectations, yet ones that are realistic and attainable. It is also the role of a parent to encourage children in their faith. Children who learn to depend on God in all life situations are equipped to be successful.

REFLECTIONS

How do I feel about the expectations I have for my child? Are some too high? Too low? Which are about right?

IMPACT MY FAMILY

Let's Talk

Today I practiced a technique of stating what I understand about situations my child may face. Look at the examples of language designed to show understanding (pages 92 and 93). What is your opinion of this technique? Share examples of ways you might offer encouragement to a child, or an adult, using this skill.

When children are experiencing a challenge, parents can offer a clear expression of understanding. Merely stating our observations and interpretations of our children's feelings can provide the clarity a child needs to plan his/her own solution. Remember that it is not up to parents to "fix" problems for children, but rather to support children as they learn to become self-directed.

BUILD RELATIONSHIPS

Let's Connect

Encourage

When we allow our toddlers and preschoolers to attempt new tasks without coddling, this encourages them to become independent and confident. Watch for things your child wants to do and provide encouragement with a calm smile or a comment such as, "I bet you can do that. Let me see you try that again. You are really trying hard."

Play a game to notice the positives in a family! Write skills, accomplishments, or positive characteristics of each family member on small pieces of paper. Place the papers in a bowl. At the dinner table, take turns pulling out a paper, reading aloud, and then asking the family to guess who is being described.

Teens generally spend a lot of time in front of a mirror. Try to surprise your teen with words of encouragement written on stick-it notes and tucked on their mirror...*I love what I see when I look at you. You are created in God's image. No one thinks you are more handsome than I do.*

PRAYER REMINDERS

"Therefore **encourage** one another and
build each other up,
just as in fact you are doing."

—1 THESSALONIANS 5:11

JOSHUA

My Child is CAPABLE

IN THIS SESSION

What does my child think?

➡ I know how to get ready for school. *If Mom has a meeting, I have to wait for her to help before I start my homework.*

➡ I can plan for my needs for the weekend trip. *I need Dad to pack me for my Boy Scout trip.*

➡ I can use the resources at school to explore my college options. *My mom better hurry and investigate all the college entrance requirements.*

➡ Grandpa can count on me to help with raking the leaves. *If I don't get my chores done I will be in trouble.*

In my eyes you are capable and significant!

JOSHUA

*Deuteronomy 31,
Numbers 27:12–13,
Joshua 1–24*

The people of Israel had been following Moses for forty years. Forty years of wandering through the desert! Finally, the promised land of Canaan was in sight, but as a result of Moses' sin (Numbers 20:12), God would not allow Moses to go on. Who would be a leader to replace Moses? Joshua.

God chose Joshua, a man of faith and courage, to finish the march and conquer the land. Moses was confident that, with God's guidance, Joshua would be able to complete the task that Moses had spent his life working toward. Moses confidently announced to all the people that Joshua, a capable successor, had been chosen.

Joshua was a strong leader, but the key to his success was his submission to God. Joshua knew that God was his source of strength and courage. God filled Joshua with the spirit of wisdom, and promised to be with him always. As a result, Israel remained faithful to God throughout Joshua's lifetime.

What made Joshua feel capable of leading the people?

Read Deuteronomy 31:1–8, 14–15, and 23.

Verses 7–8

Verses 14–15

Verse 23

Read Numbers 27:12–23

Verses 16–17

Verse 20

Verses 22–23

WHEN WE CONSIDER WHAT MADE JOSHUA FEEL CAPABLE, WE GAIN INSIGHT ABOUT WHAT WILL HELP OUR CHILDREN TO FEEL CAPABLE:

People feel capable when:

- they are given clear expectations.
- someone in authority believes in them.
- they know they are needed.
- they have the skills needed to do a job.
- they are given responsibility for a task.
- someone speaks of their competence in front of others.

Can you imagine being chosen to fill the shoes of Moses? We would certainly understand if Joshua had said, "I can't! I don't think I am capable of handling this job!" But God shows us, through the life of Joshua, how to instill confidence and courage in ourselves, and in our children.

God was with Joshua, and God is capable of anything.

"Jesus looked at them and said, 'With man this is impossible, but not with God; all things are possible with God.'"
—Mark 10:27

Be Strong and Courageous... With God, you ARE ABLE!

WE ARE THE MIRRORS THROUGH WHICH CHILDREN SEE THEMSELVES

Have you ever considered that children see themselves through the messages they receive from us?

One afternoon Mom walked in to find Amanda coloring so vigorously that the marks went off the paper and onto the counter. In frustration Mom said, "You are so messy! Look at this countertop!"

As Amanda immediately burst into tears, Mom remembered, "I am a mirror." Mom said, "Here, try this spray cleaner. I'm sure you are capable of cleaning this up."

Amanda's tears stopped and she scrubbed with all her might. When the marks were removed, Amanda beamed with pride.

Young children generally believe that adults know more than they do themselves. The *opinions* we express become *fact* in the mind of an impressionable child.

A POSITIVE REFLECTION...

"And what do we teach our children in school? We teach them that two and two make four, and that Paris is the capital of France. When will we also teach them what they are? We should say to each of them: Do you know what you are? You are a marvel! In the millions of years that have passed, there has never been another child like you. You may become another Shakespeare, a Michelangelo, a Beethoven. You have the capacity for anything! Yes, you are a marvel."

–PABLO CASALS

Just as Joshua was in Moses' shadow and Joshua mirrored Moses, our children watch us and mirror us. Let them see us trusting God to make us capable.

CONTRIBUTIONS

If a child can walk, he can help pick up toys.

Responsibility for chores makes children feel capable. When very young children learn that they can do simple jobs well, they gain confidence to move on to more elaborate jobs as they grow older.

Kids want to feel useful and needed, just as adults do!

Helping with family work gives children a sense of belonging and importance. Don't think of chores as a favor a child might (or might not) do for a parent, nor as a punishment the parent has to police.

Build chores into the daily routine of all family members and know that we are empowering children with competence.

How do you allow your children to help at home?

What can be learned by pitching in?

What is keeping you from encouraging your child to help?

Do you redo your child's job? What message does this send?

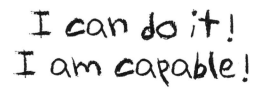

I can do it!
I am capable!

"I am a contributing member of the family!

I like having a choice in what I do to help.
Let me give this a try."

2 Year Olds

- Wipe up spills
- Pick up toys
- Spray water on windows, wipe clean
- Use dustbuster
- Dust with a cloth
- Sort dark/light clothes

3-4 Year Olds

- Sweep with a child-size broom
- Rinse fruit
- Match up socks from dryer
- Unpack groceries
- Sort recyclable items
- Put dirty clothes in hamper
- Fold washcloths

5-6 Year Olds

- Make bed
- Set table (no sharp knives)
- Help wash the dog
- Bring in the mail
- Stir ingredients for recipe
- Help shop for groceries— select good fruit

7-9 Year Olds

- Rake leaves
- Set out clothes for next day
- Scrub sinks
- Gather trash from all cans
- Take trash to curb
- Water plants
- Fold clothes and put away

10-12 Year Olds

- Do dishes
- Take care of pet
- Keep room picked up
- Vacuum
- Pack school lunch
- Make list and pack for weekend trips

Teens

- Mow lawn
- Wash car
- Pick up a few things at the store
- Do laundry
- Make a meal
- Occasionally be responsible for siblings

These are general, suggested ages. Keep in mind that every child is unique.

WHEN PROBLEMS ARISE...

What if my child says "no" to helping with the chores?

What about a child who repeatedly forgets to do his chores?

Consider this scenario:

Tuesday night kitchen clean up has been assigned to 13-year-old, Mike. The problem is that he hates clean up, and he often "conveniently" has an activity right after dinner so he "needs" to rush out of the house. His parents have tried grounding him, leaving the dishes for his return, and simply "laying down the law" but so far all they've gotten is a shouting match, an angry son, and a kitchen full of dirty dishes.

Why do parents care so much about chores? What do they want?

What information about teenagers might help parents understand Mike's perspective? (see chapter 4, page 65)

Be sure to really give up the responsibility for chores. Sometimes parents assign a job, but then nag and remind so much that kids know they don't have to remember to do it. Mom never forgets!

Until kids have responsibility for a job, they don't feel the sense of accomplishment for completing it.

WORK TOGETHER!

Here is a process for working together with Mike that will help him become more responsible and feel capable for solving his own problems.

1. Clearly state the problem
"This is how I feel about this problem...
What is the problem from your (Mike's) perspective?"

2. Brainstorm options—together
"How can we solve this problem? What are your ideas?"

3. Consider outcomes from each option
"How would that idea work out?"

4. Make a joint decision
"What do you need to give me what I need?
Can we agree to try...?"

5. State clear expectations
"What will be the consequence to each
of us if this plan falls through?"

Throughout this whole discussion remember that, as children are learning, a parent can:

- LISTEN
- SHOW UNDERSTANDING
- ASK A GOOD QUESTION TO HELP CLARIFY THE ISSUE

WHEN CHILDREN SOLVE PROBLEMS, THEY FEEL CAPABLE.

Jennifer is in the third grade and continually forgets her homework at school. Dad has been fixing this problem for her by driving back to school, and if the school is locked, writing notes to the teacher. Finally, Dad has decided to teach Jennifer to solve her own problem.

1. Clearly state the problem

"You are not remembering to bring your work home, and I am no longer willing to go get it."

2. Brainstorm options—together

"Tape a reminder note on my desk."
"Put a note in my coat pocket."
"After each class I could put my work right in my backpack."
You could still drive me back to school."

3. Consider outcomes from each option

"I'd be embarrassed to have a note on my desk."
"I might forget to look in my coat pocket."
"It's hard to find time to get to my backpack during the day."
"Dad doesn't want to be responsible for Jen's work."

4. Make a joint decision

"Let's try the coat pocket note for a week and see if it helps."

5. State clear expectations

If Jennifer forgets her work, she won't have it.
Dad won't be driving back to school anymore.

A PARENT'S WORDS
can help kids feel capable

There is a difference be-
tween praise and encouraging
kids to feel capable. Praise
is a judgment about our
child's worth. It's better
to tell our kids specifically
what positive thing we've observed.

Try to get away from praise. Encourage kids to feel proud of
their accomplishments, not merely glad that they pleased their
parent.

Which phrase in each set helps the child feel capable?

☐ "You are such a nice girl with that cat."
☐ "You pet that cat so gently."

☐ "I am so happy when you help me carry groceries."
☐ "Wow! You are strong to carry those heavy groceries."

☐ "I see that you taught your little brother how to play
a new game."
☐ "What a good brother you are!"

☐ "You are such a smart boy."
☐ "You figured out your own way to do a puzzle."

Good parenting is often a matter of
seeing capabilities in our children SO
CLEARLY that they come to see it in
themselves.

A Fairy Tale — Of Sorts

*O*nce upon a time there was a little boy named Stuart. Each morning Stuart's mother would gently turn open the blinds to let just enough light into Stuart's room, to softly nudge him awake.

Stuart would pitter patter into the bathroom and step into the nice warm shower. The water was already running – at the perfect temperature. When Stuart stepped out of the shower, every day, he found a soft warmed towel waiting for him. So cozy.

Back in his bedroom, Stuart would find his bed was already neatly made and his clothes for the day were matched and set out carefully there on his bedspread.

Once dressed, Stuart would come downstairs to the dining room and enjoy a beautiful table set with a delightful glass of freshly squeezed orange juice, two perfectly poached eggs, and whole wheat toast with homemade strawberry jam. Yum!

Mother was standing near the front window watching for the school bus. When she saw the bus come into view, she would help Stuart put on his jacket, zip it up tight to his chin, and hand him his lunch in a lovely monogrammed bag... "S" for Stuart!

Have a great day at school, Stuart!

❖   ❖   ❖

*N*ow, at this same time, just down the street, lived a little girl named Allissa.

Each morning Allissa's parents had to leave very early for their jobs. So, Allissa was accustomed to setting her own alarm clock each night before she went to sleep.

Awakening to the alarm in the morning, Allissa had learned to shower, choose her clothes for the day, pour a bowl of Rice Krispies for breakfast, prepare a sandwich for her lunch, get into her coat and hat, and make her way down to the bus stop... on time.

Well, many years passed, and by and by Stuart and Allissa became friends— good friends. In fact, they fell in love and they were married.

On one of the first Monday mornings of their married life, Allissa got up and left the house very early for her job. Stuart woke up late.

Stuart dashed into the shower and when he stepped out, dripping wet, he was dismayed to find that not only was there no WARMED towel waiting, the towel hanging there was wet! Shaking and shivering, Stuart went to find his clothes but his favorite blue shirt, which he always wore on Mondays, was in the hamper. NOW WHAT? He had to wear the yellow shirt with the rather scratchy collar.

Dashing to the dining room, Stuart pulled up a chair. He sat and waited, and waited, AND WAITED! No freshly squeezed orange juice? No poached eggs? WHERE'S MY STRAWBERRY JAM?

This was going to be a very bad day.

MY CHILD IS CAPABLE

As children are working to become independent, one thing that will serve them well is an "I can do it" attitude. We help our children see themselves as capable by giving them responsibility, teaching them how to solve their own problems, and noticing their accomplishments.

REFLECTIONS

When I consider my child on the road to feeling capable and becoming an independent human being, I think his most challenging task will be...

What specific activity can I do this week to empower him to feel successful?

IMPACT MY FAMILY

Let's Talk

This week I thought about how parents help their children feel capable.

What ideas do you have for how children can contribute to a family? What jobs do you think are appropriate for my child?

If expectations for chores in a home are left vague, or if parents disagree on the level of involvement they expect from children, this can be a point of controversy.

Have a family discussion about chores, including any children who are old enough to have an opinion about this issue. Opening communication, giving parents the chance to explain why jobs are an important part of family life, and allowing kids the opportunity to express their ideas will help the entire family work together. Kids should be allowed time to tell about the jobs they like and dislike and other requests and complaints they may have.

In the end, children will feel good knowing they were part of a family decision, rather than dumped on with some jobs!

BUILD RELATIONSHIPS

Let's Connect

Opportunities For Success

Create a "comfy couch or get better chair" where your toddler can go to calm down. You might put a soft blanket, stuffed animal, books or special toy in a basket nearby. When your child has lost control teach her how to go to that special place until she feels better and has regained control. This shows her you believe she can learn to handle their emotions. You are not mad at her; you are helping her learn the important skill of self-control.

Find an older person who can use some company. Brainstorm ways your child could be an important part of that person's life (make a check-in phone call after school, go play cards with him, assist him with something he can no longer do, show interest in his hobby). Nothing improves our self-esteem more than knowing that we are needed and that we do make a difference in this world.

Share how much money you have budgeted for this year's family vacation. Let your teen check out destination possibilities. Ask him to be sure to take time to think about what the hidden costs might be. Hold a family meeting to make this important decision based on your teen's hard work.

PRAYER REMINDERS

"With man this is impossible, but not with **God**;
all things are possible with **God**."

—MARK 10:27

NAOMI

BUILD Relationships

IN THIS SESSION

Choose to be connected

TODAY

✓ **Examine** three different parenting styles.

✓ **Recognize** both strength and flexibility in relationships.

✓ **Get ideas** for connecting with children to build relationships.

A mother, age 68, shared a lunch date with her son. They talked about his job, his plans for the future, as well as her feelings about her life's accomplishments, and her dreams for travel.

Near the end of the lunch, their waitress commented that they seemed to be having such a wonderful time together, so interested in each other—"You must be old friends."

The son replied, "This is my oldest friend; she's my mother! And we have been practicing staying connected for nearly forty years."

Imagine what this mother may have done all those years to build a lasting relationship with her son.

What will my relationship with my child be like twenty years from now?

NAOMI

Ruth
Chapters 1—4

Naomi was Ruth's mother-in-law. Even though the Bible doesn't give us many details about Naomi, we can see that Ruth loved and respected her. When Ruth's husband, Naomi's son, died, Naomi urged Ruth to return to her own mother's home in hopes of remarrying and starting a new life for herself. But Naomi's relationship with Ruth was so strong that Ruth preferred to stay with Naomi in a strange new land and endure all the hardships that came along with that. Obviously, Naomi and Ruth had quite a positive relationship.

Ruth trusted her mother-in-law to provide wisdom and good advice. Naomi could have easily convinced Ruth to live all her days caring for her, since she was a widow with no other children. But it was Naomi who arranged a second marriage for Ruth, understanding Ruth's needs. As a result of this marriage, Ruth eventually became the great-grandmother of David, an ancestor in the birth line of Jesus! Naomi's relationship with Ruth had a powerful impact.

Read Ruth Chapter 1
What evidence is there that Naomi is strong and trustworthy?

Ruth 1:6—10

Ruth 1:14—17

In the following verses, find examples of Naomi encouraging Ruth to become independent of her.

Ruth 1:8—13

Ruth 2:1—3

Ruth 3:1—5

Ruth 4:9—10

Naomi provided Ruth with a relationship that was strong and trustworthy, yet allowed her to become an independent person.

This is a model of the relationship children need with their parents; a relationship that will last a lifetime.

▼ ▼

"But Ruth replied, 'Your people will be my people and your God my God.'"
—Ruth 1:16b

3 PARENTING STYLES

Parents sometimes fall into patterns with their children, ranging from rigid closed-mindedness (call that IRON ROD parenting), to unstructured chaos (SILLY STRING parenting). A better, middle-of-the-road option (ROPE parenting) provides respectful, compassionate guidance while teaching children to think for themselves.

Laura, age 16, wants to go to an after-the-dance Prom Party.

IRON ROD: *Absolutely not! And I don't want to hear another thing about it!*

SILLY STRING: *Sure, I don't care what time you get home.*

ROPE: *Tell me more about this party.*

Keith, age 8, has been neglecting his very messy room.

IRON ROD: *Get up here right now! You won't leave this room until it's spotless. There will be no TV for you tonight.*

SILLY STRING: *I guess I'll have to clean up this room for you.*

ROPE: *Grandma will be here Friday. What kind of a plan can we make to get your room cleaned up before then?*

Teddy, age 2, routinely interrupts Mom when she's on the phone.

IRON ROD: *Leave me alone or I'll give you something to cry about!*

SILLY STRING: *Please be quiet, Teddy. Sorry, Margaret, I can't hear you. Don't cry, Teddy. What did you say, Margaret? Oh, just hang on. Here, Teddy, want a cookie?*

ROPE: *I have to make a phone call. Would you rather color or watch TV for a few minutes?*

How does each of these parenting styles affect the relationship between parent and child?

Mark each phrase as typical for IRON ROD (IR), SILLY STRING (SS), OR ROPE (R) parents:

SS Whatever.

IR Don't talk to me like that!

R Let's make a plan.

R You agreed to be home by 10, but you are late and I worried.

SS What time did you get home? I was asleep.

IR This is not open for discussion.

R Tell me what happened.

IRON ROD parents are inflexible and hard as steel to live with. Absolute authority is the goal, and they demand respect from their children. However, they forget that true respect is earned. Strict rules are in abundance and are to be obeyed because "I told you so." There is no room for mistakes in this family.

SILLY STRING parents are extremely flexible but have no strength. They try to be lots of fun, but break easily and can't be relied upon. There is no consistency, and kids are generally confused.

ROPE parents are strong, but they bend. Children are allowed "a little more rope" as they are encouraged to practice independence, but there is the security of connection through strong relationship. Mistakes are seen as opportunities to learn, and the rope is pulled in a bit when children over-extend themselves and need to re-evaluate a decision.

Which style of parenting comes most naturally to me? Which style will serve me and my children best?

BE STRONG!
Provide a reliable rope to hang onto.

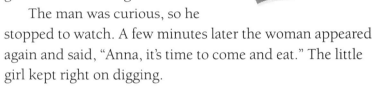

The story is told of a passerby walking down a neighborhood street, when he came upon a little girl, digging in her sandbox. Just as the man approached the little girl's house, a woman leaned out the window and said, "Anna, it's time to come and eat." But the little girl continued to dig.

The man was curious, so he stopped to watch. A few minutes later the woman appeared again and said, "Anna, it's time to come and eat." The little girl kept right on digging.

Confused, the man went closer to the little girl and said, "Excuse me, is your name Anna?"

"Yup," said the little girl.

"And, is that lady your mother?" asked the man.

"Uh huh," replied the little girl.

"Well, why haven't you gone in to eat?"

The little girl looked up and said, "She hasn't yelled yet."

IF I SAY IT,
MEAN IT!

DON'T SHOO FLIES...
FOLLOW THROUGH

Have you ever been bothered by a pesky fly? How long did you keep brushing it away, too busy or pre-occupied to get up out of your chair, find the fly swatter, and deal with this problem? Keep this analogy in mind as we consider how to be a strong, reliable parent.

"Tommy, don't bang on that coffee table with your truck! Oh dear, there's the phone. Just a minute, Tommy."

☎ *"Hello? Oh, Aunt Edna, How have you been?"*

"Tommy, I said stop banging. You'll hurt the table."

☎ *"I'm sorry Edna, what where you saying? Yes, I have been busy planning the Advent Tea at church. You know that event just gets bigger every year."*

"Tommy, that's enough banging!"

☎ *"Aunt Edna, do you know the date for that birthday lunch for Mrs. Wilson? I don't want to miss it."*

"Tommy, if you don't stop that banging you are going to your room!"

☎ *"I'm sorry Aunt Edna. Tommy just doesn't listen to a thing I say these days. What? You want an idea for a Christmas gift for him? Well, just give me a minute. It's hard to think with all this banging going on."*

"Tommy! Now look what you've done to my new table! Why are you so naughty? What will I do with you?

If parents care about stopping a behavior, they care enough to do something about it—hang up the phone and lift Tommy away from the table. If not, they need not bother to say it!

When parents follow through on what they say, children feel the security of a strong parent.

BE STRONG, yet flexible
"Give 'em a little rope!"

Sometimes when parents take time to understand the situation and their child, they choose to change their mind.

Jeremy and Dad are playing catch in the backyard. With every pitch, Jeremy also gives Dad a "pitch" for extending his curfew time.

Jeremy: *Hey, Dad, I want my Saturday night curfew to be later.*
Dad: *Later curfew is not a good idea.*
J: *Come on, Dad. My curfew is just too early.*
D: *Your curfew is just fine.*
J: *Everybody else stays out later.*
D: *You're not everybody else, are you?*
J: *Obviously not, or I'd be staying out later!*
D: *Well, you won't be staying out later!*
J: *I'm not giving up on this! I need some freedom!*
D: *Time out Jeremy! I quit... Let's talk about this curfew later.*

In this skit, Dad realized that being a strong parent doesn't always mean winning the argument. In fact, it takes a great deal of strength to be the one who stops an argument.

Sometimes parents are confused and think that being strong means they always have to be right. Families who understand the importance of relationships strive to create an atmosphere where it's not "my way" or "your way" but, working together, we'll find a "better way."

This is the challenge to parents:

Be a strong, firm foundation that children can trust, but also be flexible when you need to change your mind.

After Dad had time to cool off and collect his thoughts, he called...

Dad: *Hey, Jeremy, can we talk again about your curfew time?.*
Jeremy: *I think it should be later!*
D: *And you know how I feel about you being out too late.*
J: *I'm the only kid who has to be home at eleven o'clock!*
D: *Sounds to me like you feel embarrassed about that.*
J: *You'd be embarrassed too if your friends wouldn't even drive with you anymore because you had to leave so early!*
D: *Wow, that must be upsetting to have your friends leave you out.*
J: *And I don't get it, because our strict city curfew says midnight!*
D: *So, you feel like there's no reason for an eleven o'clock curfew.*
J: *Well, can you think of one?*
D: *I've always thought it was for your safety.*
J: *Dad, I'm just at a friend's house! We're not driving all around town!*
D: *If we can agree that you will call and let me know where you are at eleven, I guess midnight is OK with me.*
J: *Really? You changed your mind?*
D: (rather surprised) *I guess I did!*

Say no when necessary, but say yes as often as possible.
Be clear, but don't always demand my way.
Be predictable, but don't be boring.
Know what's important to me,
but understand what's important to my child.

HAVE SOME FUN! CONNECT!

Let kids bang on pots and pans
Read books out loud with joy
Surprise your children
Hug a tree
Make lots of forts with blankets
Paint together
Bake a cake and eat it with no hands
Mail letters to your kids
Take your child on a date
Paint your tennis shoes
Dance to old rock-and-roll music
Color Easter eggs in September
Discover something
Laugh a lot

Brainstorm a list of things your family can do to connect with each other. Get your child's input!

WACKY, KOOKY, CRAZY stuff our family can do:

Places we can go that are WITHIN A 1 HOUR DRIVE:

FREE things we can do:

Activities that can be completed in 1 HOUR OR LESS:

DON'T UNDERESTIMATE THE POWER OF HUMOR...

The average child laughs 400 times a day; for adults a good day is 4 or 5. Take a lesson from your child.

"The best way to keep children home is to make the home atmosphere pleasant...and let the air out of the tires."

—Dorothy Parker

WHEN WAS THE LAST TIME YOU LAUGHED OUT LOUD?

One Christmas a few years ago, I realized that our children, now growing older, weren't going to be finding toys under the Christmas tree. The gifts they would be unwrapping would be clothes, jewelry, a new wallet—all fine gifts but not as much fun to open as the toys of years past.

So, I bought five inexpensive remote-controlled cars; one for each of our three children, one for my husband, and a bright blue one for myself! These five packages, the last gifts unwrapped, gave our family something to laugh about, racing each other around the living room, into the kitchen, banging into each other, and CONNECTING!

BUILD RELATIONSHIPS

What makes some children stay in touch with their parents when they become adults? RELATIONSHIP!

Relationships are built
In an atmosphere of trust and stability;
Where children know their parents will listen
and try to understand them;
Where a family enjoys each other's company.

Relationship gives parents influence,
rather than control.
A relationship can last a lifetime.

REFLECTIONS

What will I do this week to strengthen the relationship I have with my child?

IMPACT MY FAMILY

Let's Talk

Today I had the opportunity to consider how important positive relationships are in my family. What are some things you did as a child that made you feel closer to your parents? What activities do you enjoy doing with children today?

Sometimes parents feel that they don't have enough money to do the things they want to do with their kids. It is helpful to recognize that expensive trips to Disney World are great, but the things kids remember most fondly are often simple, unexpected moments that let kids know their parents enjoy being with them.

"I remember the time my mom met us at the door with silly string and we all ran to the backyard to empty those cans on each other!" and "One winter night my dad told us to jump in the car (in our pajamas!) because we were going to find a hot fudge sundae somewhere!" are a couple of real life examples that will remain in a child's memory well into adulthood. We hope our relationships with our children will last just as long. Relationships can last a lifetime.

BUILD RELATIONSHIPS

Let's Connect

Connect

Take an extra minute when changing a diaper or giving a bath to massage your infant or toddler. Try a nice back rub or leg and arm massage. A loving touch says, "You are important to me. I have time for you."

There is an art to getting your child to talk with you. Play "talk show host" the next time you have a few minutes. Instead of saying, "How was school?" try asking a specific question. "Who did you play with at recess today?" or "What book are you reading at school?" are easier to answer and can break the ice for more in-depth conversation.

An easy way to connect with your teenager, and send the message that you care about his/her interests, is to join an activity already in progress. Rather than nagging your teen to join you in a job or game when you get home, slip in and get in sync with what your kid is already doing. Say, "Can you show me how to do that?" and watch your child's reaction!

PRAYER REMINDERS

"But Ruth replied,
  Your people will be my people and
  your God **my God.**"

—RUTH 1:16b

NEHEMIAH

Seek

INFLUENCE

Who Influences Me?

TODAY

✓ **Recognize** what makes parents influential in their children's eyes.

✓ **Consider** conse-quences.

✓ **Help kids** think and make good decisions.

DICTATOR OR **GUIDE?**

MODEL OR **CRITIC?**

LISTENER OR **LECTURER?**

ENFORCER OR **RESOURCE?**

Influential people support me to think and make my own decisions

137

NEHEMIAH

*Nehemiah
Chapters 1–13*

The city of Jerusalem had been left defenseless without strong walls to protect it. This disturbed Nehemiah, a Jew who worked as "cupbearer" to the Persian king. Nehemiah knew that God could use his talents to rebuild the walls.

The manner in which Nehemiah tackled this job shows us that he was a man of great influence. He was able to organize and motivate a large number of people to take ownership and contribute to the completion of this project. Nehemiah was a leader who delegated jobs and encouraged others to do their part. He recognized the efforts and achievements of the workers, commenting that "the people worked with all their heart." (verse 4:6) Nehemiah's influence obviously came through the way he treated the people around him.

When danger and threats appeared, Nehemiah comforted the people by challenging them to remember that the Lord would fight for them. In record time, only 52 days, the job was finished. Even Nehemiah's adversaries were amazed by this success—they recognized God's hand in Nehemiah's work.

We have been talking about how important it is to begin problem solving with our children by "clearly stating the problem." Compare this to Nehemiah's actions in verses 2:11–20.

Scan Nehemiah Chapter 3
How did Nehemiah tackle the project/problem of rebuilding Jerusalem's walls?

Read Nehemiah 6:15—16
How can this passage give comfort and encouragement to me as I consider the work of raising my children?

Nehemiah was a man of influence. He trusted God to use his skills to encourage and direct others to complete a great project. Notice that he didn't solve the problem alone—he had confidence in the abilities of others and in the power of God. When problems occur in a family, a parent doesn't have to be a SUPER-PARENT with all the answers. Parents can call on their family, especially their children, and God for help.

▼ ▼

"This work had been done with the help of our God."
—Nehemiah 6:16b

Children can think and make decisions!

Would you like to wear your pink or yellow pajamas?

Would you like to practice piano now or after dinner?

Would you like to eat beans or corn?

Parents empower their children when they trust them to make choices and decisions. However, as our children grow older, decisions appear that are more difficult to give up:

Are you sure you want to wear those plaid pants with a striped shirt to school?

Do you really want to refuse to eat this sandwich and have nothing to eat until dinner tonight?

Are you certain that you want to take the chance of getting home too late to complete your homework?

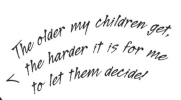

The older my children get, the harder it is for me to let them decide!

We want our children to grow to be self-disciplined, to have the ability to order themselves to do what's right!

This is a skill that develops over time, with practice.

Parents keep SOME decisions for themselves

Allowing children to think for themselves and make decisions builds important life skills, but some decisions are NOT appropriate for children.

For example, with a two-year-old, it's pretty clear that a parent would not say,

"Would you like to go to bed?" or

"Would you like to take a bath?"

Likewise, a parent of a seven-year-old would probably never say, "Would you like to do your homework tonight?" These are clear decisions that parents take charge of during the formative years.

As years pass, and children grow in their ability to think, parents need to give more decisions to them. Consider some of the decisions that were inappropriate for young children, applied to teenagers:

"Would you like to go to bed?"

"Would you like to take a bath?"

"Would you like to do your homework tonight?"

They seem rather silly, don't they?

Teenagers need to take control of their own schedule and make decisions for themselves. Parents who allow children to make age-appropriate decisions all along the way have laid the groundwork so that by the time kids get to be teens, they are making most of their own decisions. It takes lots of practice to become skilled in making good decisions.

Parents can be Children's Most Influential Teachers...

Lisa: Mom, you know that new red shirt of mine?

Mom: The one you are going to wear for our family Christmas photo?.

L: Yes, well, I loaned it to Jennifer and she lost it.

M: What? That was so expensive! I can't believe you let her borrow it!

L: She needed a special shirt for a party.

M: So you let her take that one? You don't value your things. That's it! No clothing allowance for one month!

L: I already feel terrible about my shirt. Why are you trying to make me feel worse?

M: You have to learn a lesson. You can't keep being so irresponsible with your things.

L: I have learned one thing today—never tell your mother anything.

M: I'm just telling you that sometimes you just don't think!

L: You don't know what I think!

Mom thought... "It's my responsibility to teach Lisa the value of money. I want to raise Lisa to respect me and the things I do for her."

Lisa thought... "Mom doesn't understand what it's like to be my age and have friends. In the future, I had better keep my problems to myself."

What was Mom trying to teach? What did Lisa learn? What kept Mom from being a positive influence for Lisa?

There is a better way! A more influential way!

Teach Kids to Solve Problems

"When Lisa has a problem, I want her to learn that what she needs is a good plan, not a good excuse."

1. Clearly State the Problem

Lisa doesn't have a shirt for the family photo.

2. Brainstorm Solutions Together

Ask Jennifer to replace it.
Lisa could replace it.
Mom could replace it.
Lisa could wear something else for the photo.

3. Consider Outcomes from Each Option

Jennifer may get mad.
Lisa would have to do extra babysitting jobs to get money.
Mom might feel taken advantage of and angry.
Lisa won't match the rest of the family in the photo.

4. Make a Joint Decision

Lisa will earn enough money to buy a new one.

5. State Clear Expectations

Lisa will have a shirt in hand one week before the photo.
If Lisa doesn't earn the money she needs by one week before the photo, she will give up her weekend to stay home and work odd jobs, earning money to buy the new shirt.

What did Lisa learn through this process?

Clear expectations include a discussion about CONSEQUENCES.

Some decisions result in NATURAL CONSEQUENCES: things that just happen naturally with no intervention.

- **If you don't eat your school lunch, you will be awfully hungry when you get home.**
- **If you don't wash your hair tonight, you will have to go to school with dirty hair tomorrow.**

NATURAL

In the situation with Lisa and the lost red shirt, the NATURAL CONSE-QUENCE would have been that Lisa would have worn something else and not matched the rest of the family in their Christmas photo. Sometimes the natural consequence is not acceptable; sometimes it is unsafe. In the case of the Christmas photo, Mom probably cared about having the family match in the photo, and so that was not an option.

When natural consequences are not acceptable, families can discuss what a MEANINGFUL CONSEQUENCE would be. This type of consequence gives the child ownership for the problem, and the opportunity to fix it.

- **If you spill your juice, you'll get a paper towel and wipe it up.**
- **If you hit your playmate, you will have to stop playing and come sit down with me.**
- **If you come home after curfew, I won't be able to trust you to go out next weekend.**

Lisa and her mother determined a MEANINGFUL CONSEQUENCE that was clear. Lisa has the opportunity to earn money to buy a new shirt, but if that doesn't work out, and she comes up short, she agrees to give up her weekend, staying home to do some extra chores for her parents to earn the money she needs. Since this is clear, and stated ahead of time, there should be no shaming or anger involved if the situation ends up that way.

MEANINGFUL

How do parents and kids determine consequences?

First, parents must believe that the reason for determining a consequence is to help a child learn to be responsible; it is not to "slap on a punishment" when a parent is angry.

Consequences are determined through discussion, not in the heat of an argument. Then, the focus changes from "My parent did this to me" to "I made a decision to go against what we discussed and now my parent and I are following through with the consequence we discussed."

The opportunity for discussion, joint decision-making, and following through helps parents gain influence and respect with their children.

Is this a NATURAL CONSEQUENCE? or a MEANINGFUL CONSEQUENCE?

☐ If you don't wear mittens, your hands will be cold.

☐ If you don't wear mittens, you won't be able to play outside.

☐ I you leave your pajamas on the wet bathroom floor, you will help me do a load of laundry when you come home from school instead of going outside to play.

☐ If you leave your pajamas on the wet bathroom floor, you will have wet pajamas tomorrow night.

☐ If you lose your baseball glove, you won't have one.

☐ If you lose your baseball glove, you will have to buy a new one with your savings money.

☐ If you go to bed late, you will be tired in the morning.

☐ If you hit your classmates, they won't want to play with you.

☐ If you don't pick up your toys, I will take them away for one week.

☐ If you play in the front yard, where I don't think it's safe, you will have to come inside the house.

Work Together to Solve Problems

1. Clearly State the Problem

2. Brainstorm Solutions Together

3. Consider Outcomes from Each Option

4. Make a Joint Decision

5. State Clear Expectations, With an Agreed-Upon Consequence

Teach kids HOW to think, not WHAT to think.

SEEK INFLUENCE

Parents want to be the people their children turn to for guidance. They want children to trust their judgement and listen to their advice. Parents want influence!

No parent can demand influence. Influence comes because our children care about us and about what we think. This is the result of a relationship where parents understand children and their challenges and encourage them to learn to make decisions.

REFLECTIONS

What is one thing I can do this week to encourage my child to think for himself and make decisions?

IMPACT MY FAMILY

Let's Talk

Today I thought about helping my child learn to make his own decisions.

What decisions were your responsibility when you were my child's age? How does that compare with the decisions my child makes today?

In all of life, people need to identify problems, generate ideas that could be solutions, and make decisions. Helping our children practice these skills is not just a discipline strategy to make our parenting more effective. When young children think and make decisions, they are practicing skills that will help them to become self-disciplined and more confident as they grow older.

When we ask our children, "What do you think?" we limber up their brains and let them know we value their opinions.

BUILD RELATIONSHIPS

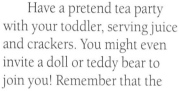

Let's
Connect

Think Together

Have a pretend tea party with your toddler, serving juice and crackers. You might even invite a doll or teddy bear to join you! Remember that the best part of a tea party is the conversation, so ask "social" questions about how he is enjoying the food and the weather. Watch your toddler imitate the way you sip your tea, use your spoon, and carry on a conversation. Lots of thinking and learning will be going on at this party!

Share things that are in your imagination! When reading a story together stop and ask, "What do you think might happen next?" Then take a moment to share your ideas. Questions like this, which have no right or wrong answer, give parents a glimpse inside a child's creative mind and help families connect by sharing fantasy.

When you are driving in the car with your teenager, steer her down memory lane with you. Start talking about the day you got your driver's license, your first car, or what you and your friends did on Friday nights. Can you recall things that seem like a history lesson to your teen? How about popcorn without a microwave? Writing a paper without a computer? Telephones without voice mail? Music without CD's?

PRAYER REMINDERS

**"This work had been done,
with the help of our God."**

—NEHEMIAH 6:16b

MARY

Take Another PERSPECTIVE

✓ **Acknowledge** and express our own feelings.

✓ **Take** a child's point of view.

What do you see?

A lovely young woman with a feather in her hair or an old woman with a big nose and a scarf over her head?

✓ **Get** kids talking.

We all see things differently. Effective parents try to understand their own perspective, as well as that of their child.

MARY

Luke 2:41–52

Mary, the mother of Jesus, her husband, Joseph and her son, Jesus, had journeyed to Jerusalem to attend a great festival. It was customary for those attending these festivals to travel together in caravans, with the women and children at the front of the caravan, and the men bringing up the rear. Since Jesus was 12 years old, he could have been in either group. Both Mary and Joseph could have assumed that Jesus was traveling with the other, not noticing his absence for several days.

However, Jesus was not with the caravan at all. He had stayed behind in Jerusalem, absorbed in discussion in the temple courts, a famous place of learning. The greatest rabbis would have been gathered there to teach and discuss truths. The coming Messiah would no doubt have been a popular discussion topic. Is it any wonder that Jesus would have been eager to listen and to share his wisdom?

This story presents an example of Mary needing to understand an incident from her Child's perspective.

Read Luke 2:41–52
How do you think Mary and Joseph felt those three days when they were looking for Jesus?

Re-read verse 48.
What was Mary's perspective on Jesus' disappearance? How would I have felt in the same situation?

In a difficult situation, it's often our first reaction to say that we are angry with a situation or a person—perhaps our child! As we "dig deeper" we often discover that we aren't angry, but rather afraid, hurt, embarrassed, or worried. Identifying those primary emotions can be helpful in working to a solution.

Re-read verse 49.
What was Jesus' perspective about being away from his parents?

Realize that at 12 years old, this was Jesus' first opportunity to be among scholarly people who where discussing God, His Father! Can you understand why Jesus thought he was right to stay in the temple?

When problems occur it is important to listen and attempt to understand the situation from the other person's point of view. What insights does this give us about parent/child relationships?

▼ ▼

"My dear brothers, take note of this: Everyone should be quick to listen, slow to speak and slow to become angry."
—James 1:19

Dig deeper to understand
MY FEELINGS

Why do I care so much?

Remember that anger is a secondary emotion. Several parents took the time to figure out their real feelings, and this is what they realized:

Sometimes I get so ANGRY when my child misbehaves!	How do I really feel?
I've tried everything and nothing worked!	Hopeless
I have so much to do and never seem to have time for myself!	Trapped
I take it personally when my child "vents" on me!	Attacked
He acts out when other people are watching and judging me!	Embarrassed
I don't know what to do with her!	Inadequate
What if he gets into trouble and "turns out bad?"	Worried
He doesn't seem to respect me.	Threatened

When parents take the time to identify real feelings, they generally realize that they're not MAD, even though that's what they say. Real feelings are deeper and take more time to understand.

Express my feelings with an "I MESSAGE."
How can I express these feelings without making the situation worse?

I feel _____ when _____ because _____ .

The mom of Carrie, a 6-year-old, shared that she was beside herself with anger most days! Carrie watched way too much TV. She was constantly tormenting her 3-year-old brother. Barbie dolls, markers, and games were strewn all over the house. Carrie was always begging for a ride to her best friend's house.

On top of this, Mom was trying to keep up with the laundry, carpools, cooking, cleaning, volunteering at school, and a part-time job. She was so mad at Carrie for not helping her, but instead making more work for her.

After taking time to identify and understand her true feelings, Mom realized that she wasn't mad at her daughter. She was overwhelmed because she never got a break to do anything for herself, or anything fun with her children.

Mom tried expressing her feelings to her daughter by saying, "Carrie, I feel overwhelmed when I have so much work to do because it leaves me no time to sit and play with you."

An "I MESSAGE" helped clarify the real issue so Mom and Carrie could begin to work together on a solution, without anger.

Think of a time when I seemed really angry! What was I really feeling? Write an "I MESSAGE."

Keep digging to get to the bottom of the situation from my

CHILD'S POINT OF VIEW

Where is this coming from?

How old is she? What do I know about this age?

How does her temperament affect her reactions?

What is happening in her life at this time? How are things with her schedule, friends, health, and changes?

How can I get her talking so I can learn more?

When faced with a challenge, try to dig deep enough to see life through a child's eyes.

BEHAVIORS ARE OFTEN NOT WHAT THEY SEEM.

Look at these situations from a child's perspective.

Sassy Mouth

You don't have time to listen to me. This sassing seems to get your attention.

Screaming in the Grocery Cart

I can't sit still for a 45-minute shopping trip.

Crying in the Car Seat

This is too many errands, Mom.

Fighting

No one has taken the time to show me a better way to deal with my anger.

Slamming Doors

Kids made fun of me at recess today.

Never Wanting to be Home

My friends understand me.

Not Doing Homework

I want to be independent and control my schedule.

Staying in Room

All I hear around here is what I'm doing wrong: pick up your clothes, you're late for dinner, look at your mess.

Things become more clear and my response is softened when I dig deep enough to see my child's perspective.

WHAT'S A PARENT TO DO?

Thomas, age 6, runs into the kitchen sobbing,

"Brian came to play in my tent but he didn't really play! He just knocked it down and ripped it apart! It's totally wrecked now! He did it on purpose just to be mean! I hate him!"

Consider my gut-reaction to this situation, pretending that Thomas is my child. What would I want to do or say?

Will my reaction help Thomas solve his problem?

How would the discussion with Thomas be different if all I could do was

- **Listen,**
- **Show understanding, and**
- **Ask a good question?**

"GET KIDS TALKING"
to understand a child's perspective

LISTEN Listening means just being there and letting our children know that we're paying attention. It is *not* offering opinions, suggestions, or judgements.

- *I see.*
- *Hmmm.*
- *Wow.*
- *Oh!*

SHOW UNDERSTANDING Even if I don't understand everything about the situation and my child's perspective, I can make a comment to let my child know what I DO understand.

- *Wow, something's really got you upset.*
- *That must have been...*
- *It seems to me that you think...*
- *It sounds to me like you are feeling...*
- *You sound...*

ASK A GOOD QUESTION
Use and open-ended question to get more information.

- *What happened?*
- *What's your idea?*
- *What are your options?*
- *Is there anyone else who can help?*
- *What is your first step?*
- *Say more about that.*

When children feel listened to and understood, they begin to calm down and are able to think about what to do next.

When parents do the difficult work of listening, rather than offering opinions and judgements, they are often amazed at the skill and capability of their children!

LISTENING CAN BE HARD!

It's easy to listen when our child is sad because a neighbor ruined his tent. Try using these same skills, (LISTEN, SHOW UNDERSTANDING, and ASK A GOOD QUESTION), with a more challenging scenario.

Before saying anything, don't forget to DIG DEEPER to understand myself and my child's perspective.

Kyle, age 9, and Aaron, age 6, went outside to play soccer, but Kyle merely taunted Aaron. A brotherly game of soccer had turned into "Keep-the-ball-away-from-Aaron!" When Kyle knocked down Aaron and then kicked the ball right at his stomach, Aaron burst into tears and headed to find Mom. Kyle was right behind him shouting, "OK, Mom! Here we go again! You're going to baby that brat and blame me! I hate Aaron and I hate you!"

FIRST DIG DEEPER
What might Mom be really feeling?
Why does she care so much?
Where is Kyle's behavior coming from? Age? Temperament? Life situations?

WHAT MIGHT MOM SAY?

I feel _____ when _____ because _____ .

LISTEN
Hmmm. Wow.

SHOW UNDERSTANDING
That must have been...

ASK A GOOD QUESTION
What's your idea?

A Father Listens

I wanted to listen when my son was upset, but his shouting at me was too much! I took each argument personally and generally ended up joining in the shouting match. I couldn't let him think that it was OK to talk to me like that!

I now realize that it's not about me. Listening means hearing the hard stuff, as well as the good stuff. I have learned to listen for understanding, which often means listening beyond words to hear his true heart. When he lashes out at me, it is usually the by-product of something else that's going on in his life, sometimes related to me and something I did, but often it has nothing to do with me. I'm just the closest person, and the safest target. I know that if I can stand by him and keep listening, I will learn volumes about what is going on in his world. As a parent, that is important information for me.

On a positive note, bit by bit we are working together to help him understand what he is really upset about, and how he can more tactfully express those feelings. And, I'm learning to tell him how I feel if he says mean things to me. He's learning a lot about himself, and how his outbursts affect those around him. This is one of his hardest, but most important, life lessons.

Get a child talking even if it means withholding retaliation to just listen. Parent effectiveness often comes more from what we hear than from what we say.

TAKE ANOTHER PERSPECTIVE

An old pastor's wife once told me that when she was young and had her first child, she didn't believe in striking children, although spanking kids with a switch pulled from a tree was standard punishment at the time. But one day when her son was four or five, he did something that she felt warranted a spanking—the first of his life. And she told him that he would have to go outside by himself and find a switch for her to hit him with.

The boy was gone a long time. And when he came back in, he was crying. He said to her, "Mama, I couldn't find a switch, but here's a rock that you can throw at me."

All of a sudden the mother understood how the situation felt from the child's point of view—that if my mother wants to hurt me, then it makes no difference what she does it with; she might as well do it with a stone. And the mother took the boy onto her lap and they both cried. Then she laid the rock on a shelf in the kitchen to remind herself forever: think of life from a child's perspective.

REFLECTIONS

Recall a disagreement I have had with my child. Put myself in his/her shoes and try to understand another side of the argument.

What will I do with this new understanding?

IMPACT MY FAMILY

Let's Talk

Today I considered that when there are challenges in a family it is helpful to examine the situation from the perspective of my child, as well as myself.

What situations have you observed lately that were complicated because of differing points of view?

Since, no two people are exactly alike, even within a family, there are bound to be different perspectives. When we accept this, it is easier to understand the behaviors of those we live with.

Children often disagree with their parents about rules. Try this game with your family to make it easier to see both sides of an argument:

Choose one rule that causes arguments. For example, "How late should children stay up on school nights?" Ask a child's opinion of the rule. Ask the child to give at least two reasons for this opinion. Coming up with pro and con arguments is an excellent way to help children learn to consider alternatives before making decisions. While the child is working on these pro and con arguments, parents do the same. Explain each point of view. Talk over differing opinions. Does everyone have good points? Do any rules need to be changed?

For older children, reverse roles and ask them to pretend they are the parent, while the parent pretends to be the child. Does that change opinions?

BUILD RELATIONSHIPS

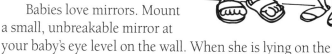

Let's Connect

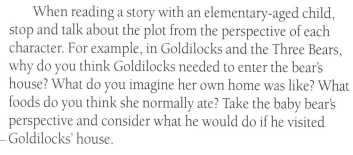

Share Perspectives

Babies love mirrors. Mount a small, unbreakable mirror at your baby's eye level on the wall. When she is lying on the floor, place her in front of the mirror and watch how she "makes friends" with that baby in the mirror!

When reading a story with an elementary-aged child, stop and talk about the plot from the perspective of each character. For example, in Goldilocks and the Three Bears, why do you think Goldilocks needed to enter the bear's house? What do you imagine her own home was like? What foods do you think she normally ate? Take the baby bear's perspective and consider what he would do if he visited Goldilocks' house.

For a fun family evening, purchase three or more different brands of cola drinks. With a black marker, label paper cups: #1, #2, and #3. Allow each family member to taste test the three drinks and vote to select their favorite. Talk about the different choices expressed in your family, realizing that a family is made up of several people who all think a little bit differently. What other things do you agree or disagree on? If you're having fun with this, try a breakfast cereal challenge, or an ice cream challenge... be creative!

PRAYER REMINDERS

"My dear brothers, take note of this:
Everyone should be quick to listen,
slow to speak and slow to become angry."

—JAMES 1:19

HANNAH

LET GO and TRUST GOD

✓ **View**
the task of parents to teach children to become independent of us, yet dependent on God.

O nce upon a time there were Three Little Pigs who lived with a wonderful Mama Pig. Through the years Mama Pig had enjoyed her Little Pigs so much: that first oink, their delight at the slop trough, and rolling about in the comfort and safety of the family mud puddle.

Day by day Mama gave her Piglets more responsibilities. Fred kept the mud puddle damp and gooey. Charlie scavenged for new corn cobs to chomp. And Alex was best at providing back scratches for the whole family. Three different Piglets; three different personalities!

✓ **Practice**
the skills presented throughout this series.

One spring day it was with bittersweet pride that Mama noted changes occurring in her Piglets. Mama had always provided opportunities for the Piglets to feel capable, fix their own mistakes, and solve their own problems. Now it was clear that they were ready to leave home and become independent of Mama. Mama trusted that her years of parenting had encouraged her Piglets to become capable and resourceful Hogs.

Parenting is a process of learning to let go of our children so they can grow up to be independent of us, but teaching them to always be dependent on God.

HANNAH

*1 Samuel
Chapters 1 and 2*

Hannah desired to have a child, but for a long time she remained childless and endured the ridicule that accompanied being barren during that time. Finally her prayer was that if God would give her a child, she promised to give the child back to the Lord for his whole life.

Samuel was born to Hannah and, as soon as he was weaned, Hannah kept her promise to God and took Samuel to the tabernacle to live with Eli. Since the customary age for weaning during those days was about three years old, we can imagine that Hannah had three years before letting Samuel go.

Hannah's story shows us that all we have is on loan from God, even our children. Hannah entered motherhood prepared to do what all parents must do—let go of their children. Hannah is a model for parents of how trusting in God can help us let go.

Read 1 Samuel Chapter 1
How did Hannah know she could depend on God with Samuel's life?

What things did Hannah do to develop such great trust in God?

Imagine what went on during Samuel's early years of life with his mother, Hannah.

If I found myself in Hannah's situation, what things would I be sure to teach my child before letting him/her go live at the tabernacle?

Hannah let her young son, Samuel, go live with Eli because she knew that was God's will. We are generally not asked to let go of our children at such a young age, but it is our job to let go eventually. Hannah could separate from Samuel because she knew he was not alone. Her faith in God comforted her to know that even though she could not be with Samuel all the time, God would never leave Samuel. We can have that same comfort as we watch our children grow. We can confidently say, "God will be with my child every day throughout his whole life."

▼ ▼

"Trust in the Lord with all your heart and lean not on your own understanding; in all your ways acknowledge Him and He will make your paths straight."
—Proverbs 3:5–6

How do I know I can depend on God?
Realize who God is!

God is described in many ways. Look at some of the different names and phrases that are used throughout the Bible to help us realize who He is. God is bigger than I can imagine! Have I experienced God in any of these ways?

Author of life
Bread of life
Eternal life
Firstborn over all creation
Friend of sinners
God of all the earth
Great Shepherd of the sheep
Judge of the living and the dead
King of kings
Light of the world
Lord of lords
God and Savior Jesus Christ
Our Peace
Resurrection and the life
Rock of ages
Teacher
The Beginning and the End
The One and Only
The Truth
The Way
Wonderful Counselor
Word of God
Glorious Crown
Master in heaven

Refuge for His people
Refuge for the oppressed
Refuge for the poor
Shade from the heat
Shelter from the storm
Source of strength
Ever present help in trouble
Builder of everything
Creator of heaven and earth
Father
God of gods
God my Maker
God of hope
Great and awesome God
My Comforter in sorrow
My Help
My hiding place
My song
Only wise God
Compassionate and gracious God
The living Father
The potter
Spring of living water
Alpha and Omega

What have I seen in my life that encouraged me to depend on God? Share specific experiences in a thanksgiving prayer.

Dear God, Thank you for experiences that have taught me I can depend on you: _____
_____ , *Amen.*

God will direct our path
How can I help my child learn to depend on God?

- Live what I believe. Model my faith.
- Encourage questioning about God as necessary; doubt should not be avoided.

- Provide opportunities for my child to build personal relationships among peer and adult spiritual role models.
- Relate spiritually to daily life in conversation.
- Don't feel I need to have all the answers. Search together to understand.

"Trust in the Lord with all your heart and lean not on your own understanding; in all your ways acknowledge Him and He will make your paths straight."
—Proverbs 3:5–6

What do I do in my family to teach my children to **depend** on God?

I'VE LEARNED — I CAN — I WILL

Mom and Sarah, age 9, are making their way through the gardening store, buying things they need to plant a new flower bed. Sarah is being sassy...

Sarah: *Don't tell me we are going down one more aisle! I promised Beth I would play today!*

Mom: *Sorry, but you won't be able to play until we get these flowers planted.*

Sarah: *Do the garden yourself! Why do I have to be the one to plant your flowers?*

Mom: *The flowers are for our family and you are part of that family.*

Sarah: *I have a life though—unlike you, obviously!*

Look at the checklist on the following page. Which of these skills will help Sarah's mother in this situation?

After taking a moment to sit down with a hot cup of coffee, Sarah's mom scribbled this note in her journal:

When I stopped to understand why I cared so much about Sarah's sassing, I realized that I would NEVER have talked back to my parents like this. I respected my parents. It feels like I must be doing something bad as a parent to have raised a child to act this way toward me. I also feel unloved when Sarah gets so angry with me, and that really hurts.

From Sarah's point of view, I understand that she had other ideas about her day, and that at age 9, she still isn't very good at disagreeing in a tactful way. I know she is capable of learning that skill, and I am glad to be the one to help her learn. I will talk with Sarah, sharing how her behavior made me feel: **"I feel disrespected when you sass me because that's not a kind way to tell me what you think."** *I'm looking forward to talking calmly with Sarah this evening when I tuck her into bed.*

☒ CHECKLIST FOR SUCCESS

☐ **UNDERSTAND MY OWN FEELINGS**
Why do I care so much?

☐ **SEE FROM MY CHILD'S POINT OF VIEW**
Where is this coming from?
Consider age, temperament, and life situation.

☐ **GET KIDS TALKING** so parents can learn more.
Listen.
> *I see. Hmmm. Wow. Oh!*

Show understanding.
> *It seems to me that you think...*
> *That must have been...*

Ask a good question.
> *What are your options?*
> *What is your first step?*

Express my feelings.
> *I feel ___ when ___ because ___.*

☐ **SEE KIDS AS CAPABLE** of solving problems.
How can my child learn he is capable?

☐ **BUILD RELATIONSHIPS** on trust and understanding.
How will this affect my relationship with my child?

☐ **WORK TOGETHER** teaching kids to think and make decisions.
Ask your child, *"What are your ideas?*
Let's discuss the consequences."

- Clearly state the problem.
- Brainstorm solutions together.
- Consider outcomes from each option.
- Make a joint decision.
- State clear expectations with agreed-upon consequences.

Consider a challenging situation in your own family. Which of these strategies will be useful?

I'VE LEARNED — I CAN — I WILL

Help Wanted: Parent

Teach Children to be Independent of Us.

Teach Children to be Dependent on God.

THE JOB OF PARENTS IS TWO-FOLD

It is a parent's job to let go so children can become independent adults. We've talked about helping our children see themselves as capable, learning to solve their own problems. Children can only become self-disciplined when their parents give them opportunities to try to direct themselves.

We teach children to become independent, but we know that throughout life children, and adults, need to rely on God. An important part of a parent's job is to share faith and teach dependence on God.

ATTITUDE FOR INDEPENDENCE

A parent's attitude can encourage independence, or show hesitancy. Which statement in each pair is most like me?

I want my child to learn self control.
I think it's my job to control my child's life.

I believe my child is capable.
I'm not sure my child can handle this.

My child can learn to solve problems.
I don't want my child to make a wrong decision.

When my child misbehaves, I want her to learn to respond differently.
When misbehavior occurs, I want to stop it at all costs.

Even though some days are challenging, I value these years when I can influence my child.
I'm overwhelmed and irritated by the demands of parenting.

ATTITUDE FOR DEPENDENCE ON GOD

The attitudes of a parent toward faith can encourage children to depend on God.

• **I know how important it is to model my faith for my child.**

• **I am glad when my child shares questions about God, even if it means she disagrees with me.**

• **I encourage my child to have relationships with other kids and adults who are spiritual role models.**

• **I talk about my faith in daily conversation.**

• **I don't have all the answers but am eager to search with my child to learn.**

One mom said it this way:

"I think that as a parent I'm supposed to work myself out of a job!"

Job Application Form

Convince an "employer" that I have credentials to be a parent who encourages both independence from me, and dependence on God. Give specific examples from my own family.

What do I do to encourage my child to be independent? _____
_____
_____

What do I do to teach my child to depend on God? _____
_____
_____

LET GO AND TRUST GOD

When you were very small
You were comforted by the security of a flannel blanket
Snugly wrapped around you.
That blanket, along with my tight caress in a rocking chair,
Could soothe you to sleep.

As years went by, you grew
And had to stretch your arms and legs.
You gripped my hand
To cross a busy street to the playground.
But as soon as we were safely on the other side,
I needed to let you go to run and climb and swing.

Today you are stretching again,
Thinking for yourself and making decisions.
I am here to encourage and love you
As you try out your own ideas.
Lightening my hold, and loosening my grip,
Gives you space to grow and discover your own strengths.

I will never let go
Of my memories of those rocking chair and playground days.
As I let go of the child you once were,
I embrace the person you are becoming,
And the relationship we will have for life.

Perhaps I will be able to do this since
I know God is here holding you and He will
never let you go.
He will guide you while
You become the person He has had in mind,
Since those days in the rocking chair.

REFLECTIONS

Write about some significant aspect of my parenting I have considered during this series.

IMPACT MY FAMILY

Let's Talk

Today I had the opportunity to consider that it is my job as a parent to reach my children to become independent of me, yet remain dependent on God.

What experiences did you have that taught you to depend on God?

Parenting strategies in this series are designed to help parents give children responsibility, encourage them to think, and teach them to solve their own problems. All of these skills will guide children to become independent of their parents.

Children need to become independent of their parents, but they must know that they can always depend on God. There are moments in life that affirm for us that God is real, loving, and often our only source of comfort and guidance. It's not uncommon for those moments to come during a crisis, a death, or relocation. At times like these we realize that it is not possible for anyone other than God to help us.

Every parent would like to shield children from painful life experiences, but we know we don't have the power to do that. However, we do have the power to teach our children how to handle such pain, by turning to God.

BUILD RELATIONSHIPS

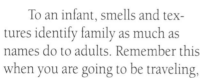

Let's Connect

Family Identity

To an infant, smells and textures identify family as much as names do to adults. Remember this when you are going to be traveling, relocating, or going to a new babysitter's home. Bring along your infant's own crib sheet or blanket to make relaxing and falling asleep easier. Babies know the smell of their family, and that smell can bring comfort in a strange place.

Share stories of family lore to give your children connections to generations past. Where did your early ancestors live? What risks did they take? What things did they value? Let children hear stories about the Grandfather who was willing to move to a new country in the hope of providing a better life for his grandchildren. Tell about the Grandmother who begged to go to school but had to stay home and help on the farm, and then lived her life encouraging her own children with a love for education.

Even when teenagers seem to want to spend every waking minute with their friends, they appreciate family connections. It is grounding to have traditions that let teens know they belong to a special family. Does your family always eat pancakes on Sunday morning? Does Dad always tell dumb jokes in the car? Is there always chocolate ice cream in the freezer? Look hard to learn what things your teen treasures about your family.

PRAYER REMINDERS

"Trust in the Lord with all your heart and
lean not on your own understanding;
in all your ways acknowledge him
and he will make your paths straight."

—PROVERBS 3:5–6

INDEX

To order additional copies of this book
or the corresponding Leader's Guide contact:

Family Impact
P. O. Box 3963
Naperville, IL 60567

www.FamilyImpact.net